BOLD
BRAVE
AND
BORN TO LEAD

BOLD
BRAVE
AND
BORN TO LEAD

Major General Isaac Brock and the Canadas

Mary Beacock Fryer

A BOARDWALK BOOK
A MEMBER OF THE DUNDURN GROUP
TORONTO

Copy-Editor: Jennifer Bergeron
Design: Jennifer Scott
Printer: Webcom

National Library of Canada Cataloguing in Publication Data

Fryer, Mary Beacock, 1929-
Bold, brave, and born to lead: Major General Isaac Brock and the Canadas/
      Mary Beacock Fryer.

Includes bibliographical references and index.
ISBN 1-55002-501-5

1. Brock, Isaac, Sir, 1769-1812 — Juvenile lierature. 2. Canada — History — War of 1812 —
Juvenile literature. 3. Canada — History — 1791-1841 — Juvenile literature. 4. Generals —
Canada — Biography — Juvenile literature. 5. Lieutenant governors — Canada — Biography —
Juvenile literature. I. Title.

FC443.B76F79 2004   j971.03'2'092   C2003-907197-9

1   2   3   4   5   08   07   06   05   04

We acknowledge the support of the **Canada Council for the Arts** and the **Ontario Arts Council** for our publishing program. We also acknowledge the financial support of the **Government of Canada** through the **Book Publishing Industry Development Program** and **The Association for the Export of Canadian Books**, and the **Government of Ontario** through the **Ontario Book Publishers Tax Credit** program, and the **Ontario Media Development Corporation's Ontario Book Initiative**.

                              J. Kirk Howard, President

Printed and bound in Canada.♾
Printed on recycled paper.

www.dundurn.com

Dundurn Press   Dundurn Press
8 Market Street, Suite 200   2250 Military Road
Toronto, Ontario, Canada   Tonawanda NY
M5E 1M6   U.S.A. 14150

TABLE OF CONTENTS

MAPS

(all maps by Geoff Fryer)

ACKNOWLEDGEMENTS

Ricky Allen, Priaulx Library, St. Peter Port, Guernsey
Brockville Museum staff: Bonnie Burke,
Curator/Director, and Larry Smith,
Volunteer Archivist
Douglas M. Grant, Brockville historian
Wayne Kelly, Plaque Program Coordinator,
Ontario Heritage Foundation
Brendan Morrissey, National Army Museum,
London, U.K., for officers' pay
Peter Twist, Kitchener, for major generals' uniform
Gavin K. Watt, Museum of Applied Military History
Gillian Reddyhoff, Curator, Ontario Government
Art Collection
Jennifer Bergeron, Dundurn Press
Jennifer Scott, Dundurn Press
Georffrey R.D. Fryer, husband and best friend,
for the maps and the endless encouragement

PREFACE

Some readers might say, "Another book about the War of 1812?" or "Another book about Sir Isaac Brock?" Why not? Perhaps I have something different to say. We have recent books on the war — by Pierre Berton and Wesley Turner, for example. The only recent study of Brock is Begamudré's book *Isaac Brock: Larger Than Life*, published in 2000, in which he conjures up a fiancée, a daughter of Aeneas Shaw named Susan.

Despite his denial, this puts Begamudré into the realm of historical fiction. I agree with C.P. Stacey, who wrote the piece on Brock in the *Dictionary of Canadian Biography*, that there is no evidence on what ladies Brock might have been romancing in Upper Canada. That is not to deny he enjoyed the company of women, partying, and dancing. If he had a serious attachment and was entirely discreet about it, more power to him.

This work is a military history of a military man. Military history does not loom large in most historical writing for young adults.

During my days at Collegiate, the Second World War was on. We had a girls' cadet corps, sister to the boys' corps, where we turned out smartly for the annual inspection in the armories. By Grade 12 I had worked myself up to lieutenant. In Grade 13, as the regimental sergeant major, I had to "dress" the whole battalion. Later I learned that the move to RSM was a demotion, from commissioned to non-commissioned officer.

My hometown is Brockville; we were very Brock-conscious. General Brock was the name of the local chapter of the IODE. My first school was General Brock, a stone building of two storeys, with two classrooms on each storey. Prominent, next to King George V and Queen Mary, was a portrait, in profile, of General Brock.

In Court House Square is a drinking fountain of marble, above which is a bust of Brock. Halloween was an occasion for pranks. Sometimes on November 1, the police would collect the dustbin that folks with no sense of propriety had stuck over the general's head.

As I worked through the materials and the various versions of the story, I found a conflict between language usage of Brock's day and our usage nearly two centuries later. For Brock and his contemporaries, Canadian meant French-speaking. English speakers were the English or

14

Preface

Text from an article in the *Recorder and Times* by Douglas M. Grant; photo by M.B. Fryer.

*Bust of General Brock, on the green in
Court House Square, Brockville. Cast in bronze, the figure is
mounted on top of a stone base with drinking fountains on
either side. The monument was erected in 1912 as a centenary
project of the General Brock Chapter, Imperial Order
Daughters of the Empire (IODE). The sculpture was the work
of Hamilton McCarthy.*

British. People of African origin were "coloured." The Aboriginal people were Indians. First Nations is a more satisfactory term, since the name "Indian" was a mistake made by Europeans who hoped they had found the wealth of India, not an unknown stretch of two continents. I have used the terms of the time in quotes and when it is necessary for clarity.

I hope my book makes a "good read," and that young adults everywhere come to appreciate Canada's military history.

— MBF

PROLOGUE

July 1810

The bateau from Lachine rows slowly up the St. Lawrence River, past the blockhouse under construction below the village of Prescott. Standing in the bow is a tall, fair-haired, broad-shouldered man in the uniform of a brigadier general in the British army. He is en route to York, the tiny capital of Upper Canada, where he will assume command of all the soldiers in the province. As they near the pretty village of Elizabethtown, which bears the same name as the township that surrounds it, their ears are bombarded with quite unfriendly sounds. Shouts of derision compete with the stamping of feet on the boardwalks near the river and the shattering of glass. Here and there a shriek of pain echoes when a well-aimed rock strikes home.

"What can this fight be about?" the general asks.

"Sounds like the Capulets and the Montagues," murmurs Major John Glegg, his aide-de-camp.

His superior does not reply. Isaac Brock is well educated, but the other officer may be better acquainted with Shakespeare.

A passenger joins in. "If those names you mentioned, sir, mean feuding, you're correct. It's been going on ever since the government decided to move the district seat and the court from Johnstown to our village. That's two years ago, sir. People have been quarrelling over a name distinct from Elizabethtown."

"Oh," says the brigadier general. "I rather fancy Elizabethtown. My mother's name was Elizabeth. But do go on."

"Some people want Williamstown, after William Buell, who is the village's founder. Others want Charlestown, after Charles Jones, a businessman who came a few years later than Mr. Buell."

"And," adds another local man, "folks outside the village are calling it 'Snarlingtown.'"

The bateau draws in beside the small wharf. First ashore is General Brock, followed by Major Glegg. At the sight of the uniforms, and a bateau following that is occupied by troops, the furious crowd disperses and the men run north towards the King's Highway. Despite its splendid name, the road is little more than a muddy track hardly fit for wagons. Brock's escort is from the

49th Regiment of Foot. They will become known as the "Green Tigers" for the dark green facings on their scarlet coats and their ferocity. All are coming ashore long enough to have some dinner.

At a tavern kept by a local magistrate, the officers sit down to eat. The enlisted soldiers make themselves at home on the riverbank and take rations from their haversacks. Meanwhile, word of Brock's esteemed presence spreads quickly throughout the village. In due course the rival factions arrive to promote their claims. Finished with his meal, Brock listens attentively. When they pause for breath, he proposes a novel solution.

"You could choose a neutral party to honour. Would the feud end if, say, you agreed to name your lovely village after me?"

Buell and Jones look at one another, nod, and say "Yes, General," in unison.

Both are too shrewd to risk offending the newly arrived British officer charged with the task of protecting Upper Canada. The Americans are just across the river in New York State, scarcely a mile off.

And thus the early historian Thad W.H. Leavitt recorded the event in his masterly work, *History of Leeds and Grenville, Ontario From 1749 to 1879.*

At Victoria School, in the year 1941, a Grade 7 teacher, Miss Agnes Smart, used Leavitt's account to write a play for the class to perform. There was Donald R. sporting a cocked hat, sword at his side, both of cardboard. He calmed the feuding parties with his suggestion, "Why not name the town after me?"

In deciding on Brockville, for whatever reason, the folk of the village had chosen the name of Ontario's favourite hero — and they did so before the valiant Brock had performed his heroic deeds.

In due course, along came what we call the revisionists. These declared that there was no evidence that Brock had ever set foot in Brockville. They could be right, but we must not let facts get in the way of a good story.

Besides, the name Brockville was found in two letters dated before Brock had performed his first heroic deed — the capture of the American fort at Detroit. His success was greeted with cheers from the people of Upper Canada. One of the letters was to Brock from his trusted officer, Colonel Robert Lethbridge. Dated August 10, 1812, Lethbridge's letter mentioned Brockville by name. The second letter was found in the papers of Charles Jones himself, dated at Brockville on August 6, 1812. Brock actually took Detroit on August 16 after a journey by horseback, wagon, and ship that started on August 5 from York.

Brock did pass by Elizabethtown/Brockville in July 1810. Who can declare with total conviction that he did not leave the bateau after passing through water known as Buell's Bay to stretch his long limbs and dine? If no proof exists that Brock ever trod the paths of Brockville, no proof exists that he did not. However, one thing is certain. The Lethbridge and Jones letters prove that during his lifetime Brock knew about the village that bore his name.

PART I

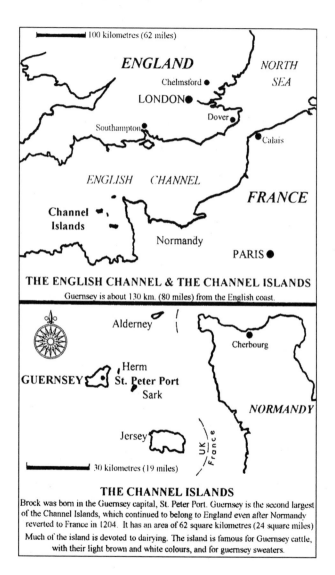

100 kilometres (62 miles)

ENGLAND

NORTH SEA

Chelmsford ●

LONDON ●

Dover ●

Southampton ●

Calais ●

ENGLISH CHANNEL

FRANCE

Channel Islands

Normandy

PARIS ●

THE ENGLISH CHANNEL & THE CHANNEL ISLANDS
Guernsey is about 130 km. (80 miles) from the English coast.

Alderney

Cherbourg ●

Herm
GUERNSEY **St. Peter Port**
Sark

NORMANDY

Jersey

UK France

30 kilometres (19 miles)

THE CHANNEL ISLANDS
Brock was born in the Guernsey capital, St. Peter Port. Guernsey is the second largest of the Channel Islands, which continued to belong to England even after Normandy reverted to France in 1204. It has an area of 62 square kilometres (24 square miles)

Much of the island is devoted to dairying. The island is famous for Guernsey cattle, with their light brown and white colours, and for guernsey sweaters.

CHAPTER ONE

Guernsey Boyhood

The future general Isaac Brock was born on October 6, 1769, at St. Peter Port on the island of Guernsey. The second largest of the archipelago, called the Channel Islands, Guernsey covers scarcely 63 square kilometres. The other islands are Jersey (the largest, at 115 square kilometres), Alderney, Sark, Herm, Jethou, and a few tiny ones. Through the north end of Guernsey the land is rocky and hilly. There the famous Guernsey cows, large with smooth coats of beige and white, were first bred. On the flatter southern part, market gardens flourished.

The countryside was laced with footpaths and tiny fields hemmed by dry stone walls. But the most important influence for the area's inhabitants was the surrounding ocean that washed over rocks exposed at low tide, alternating with long stretches of sandy beach. The historic past, stretching back more than a thousand years, has seen many chaotic events. The most recent was the German occupation during the Second World War. Since the return of peacetime, tourism has become the island's main source of wealth. It is a popular destination for those looking for a mild climate and plenty of sunshine.

The Channel Islands are different from any other place on earth. They are owned by the British monarch, but most of the people are descended from the French of Normandy. The island group was part of the duchy of Normandy in 1066, when Duke William II made his conquest of England. Then, in 1204, King Philip of France captured the mainland portion of the duchy from King John of England (the villain of Robin Hood fame). Since Philip did not succeed in laying claim to them, the Channel Islands have remained an "overseas possession" of Great Britain.

Guernsey has had lieutenant-governors, much like Canada has, who represent the monarch. The actual governing was handled by the bailiff, a chief magistrate assisted by his lieutenant-bailiff, who presided over a Norman assembly called the Royal Court of Guernsey, to which members called "jurats" were elected. The system was older than the Parliament of England, the ancestor of the Canadian Parliament. Norman French was the language of the people. By the time of Brock's birth, the people spoke a patois called *Guernesiais*. The word also refers to any person native to the island.

Unlike the majority of the island's population, the first Brock was an Englishman. Isaac's father, John, was thought to be descended from a knight, Sir Hugh Brock. During one of the territorial battles with fourteenth-century France, Sir Hugh was serving at a fort on the French coast. He escaped, reached Guernsey, and decided to put down roots there.

John (sometimes written Jean) Brock had been a midshipman in the Royal Navy. After deciding not to continue his naval career, John returned to Guernsey, and in November 1755 he married Elizabeth De Lisle, of the island aristocracy. A daughter of the lieutenant-bailiff of the bailiwick of Guernsey, Elizabeth was of Norman descent.

The Channel Islands were divided into two baili-wicks. Jersey, the largest, was one. The other was Guernsey, which included the islands of Alderney and Sark, and the much smaller Herm and Jethou. The capital was St. Peter Port, located on the east coast, overlooking one of the finest harbours in the English Channel. A sea wall and pier extended seaward from the south side of the harbour, crowned at the end by Castle Cornet. This fortress guarded the entrance to the harbour, and for centuries it housed a garrison of soldiers.

When King Henry VIII declared himself the head of the Church of England in 1531, he did not attempt to interfere with Guernsey's Roman Catholicism. The island remained part of the diocese of Coutances, France. Not until the reign of Elizabeth I did England force the Channel Islanders to leave the Church of Rome. When no French-speaking clergymen could be found in England, the Queen hired Calvinists from the French-speaking cantons of Switzerland to come to Guernsey as missionaries. As a result, the first Protestants of Guernsey were Presbyterians. By the time of Isaac Brock's birth, however, the Town Church at St. Peter Port was nominally Anglican. Guernsey was attached to the diocese of Winchester, in southern England. This accounts for certain plaques on the walls of Winchester Cathedral dedicated to the memory of people having Guernsey surnames.

The records of the St. Peter Port Town Church show that John and Elizabeth Brock had fourteen children:

Elizabeth	1756 (died at age 7)
Rebecca	1758
Jean (John)	1759
Ferdinand	1760
Pierre-Henry	1761 (died at age 2)
Daniel De Lisle	1762
William	1764
Pierre (Henry)	1765 (died at age 1)
Elizabeth 2	1767
Frederic	1768

Isaac	1769
Marie	1771
Jean-Savery	1772
Irving	1775

John and Elizabeth Brock lost a fourth child, assumed to be Rebecca, although she is not mentioned in the burial records of the Town Church. Naming a new child after one that had died was not unusual, and not regarded as a bad omen. When Isaac was born, two of his sisters and two brothers lay in the Town Church burying ground or elsewhere.

The year Isaac was seven years old, 1776, his father died, leaving ten live children and their mother, Elizabeth, to carry on. Fortunately, the family remained well-to-do, for the Brocks had always been moderately wealthy.

Isaac's first school was Queen Elizabeth College, founded by Elizabeth I in 1563, and now highly regarded. In Brock's day it was neglected and the standard of teaching was inferior. Something better was needed. His brother Daniel had been sent to Alderney to study with a Swiss pastor, M. Vallat. Afterwards Daniel went to a boarding school in Surrey, England, but when Isaac was ten the family chose for him a school in Southampton, on England's south coast. There Isaac soon had a reputation for being strong and gentle, characteristics somewhat contradictory to his accomplishments as a champion boxer. He seemed to get along well, but he was always overjoyed at holidays when he could return home to St. Peter Port.

Guernsey was a fine place to live. The sea dominated the land. The harbour was home to a large fleet of "privateers," armed ships whose commanders held permits called "letters of Marque" to prey upon ships of an enemy power. The operation of privateers was legal, if brutal. The favourite targets were merchant ships loaded with valuable goods. When sold they could make an owner very rich indeed. Young Brock had a ringside seat for viewing the comings and goings of the privateers who sought shelter from storms or made their fortunes in plain sight, selling off their booty while in port.

During Isaac's early years, Britain was usually at war with France, a favourable condition for successful privateering. In addition to the privateers, present in large numbers were the boats belonging to smugglers who talked of their business as "free trade."

Because of international tensions and trouble in the Thirteen Colonies, the British army was kept at wartime strength. The Brocks purchased a lieutenant's commission for John Junior, in the 8th (or the King's) Regiment of Foot, in 1775. The regiment was already on duty in North America, serving at outposts along the Canadian border. The following year, the second Brock son, Ferdinand, was commissioned an ensign in the 60th

(Royal American) Regiment. He, too, sailed for North America to serve against the rebels who wanted independence from Britain. Isaac decided that when his time came, he would follow Ferdinand into the army.

Young Isaac was described as a strong, healthy lad, lacking neither daring nor imagination. At age ten, one story goes, he often swam the half-mile along the seawall to Castle Cornet and back, through reefs and turbulent waters. He felt a need to explore the many islets near the harbour, sometimes swimming, at others sailing with some of his brothers in a cat-rigged dinghy with a centre board to lower or raise.

That year, tragedy struck the Brock family again. Isaac lost his second brother, Ferdinand, then serving at Baton Rouge in the Mississippi Valley. In May 1779, Spain declared war on Britain. Troops from Spanish-occupied New Orleans travelled up the Mississippi River, and by September they were laying siege to Baton Rouge. In the fighting, Ferdinand Brock, just nineteen years old, was killed. Isaac's resolve to obtain an officer's commission in a British regiment was not shaken by Ferdinand's death. If anything, he wanted more than ever to attack the foe who had deprived him of his second brother.

Isaac left his boarding school in Southampton when he was fourteen. Something had to be done about the quality of his French. In the streets of St. Peter Port and on ramblings through the lanes, shores, and fields of

Guernsey, he had acquired a knowledge of *Guernesiais*, hardly the speech of a gentleman. His brothers Daniel, now twenty-one, and William, nineteen, tracked down a French-speaking Protestant clergyman in Rotterdam, Holland, who, like Daniel's mentor, M. Vallat, was of the right language and the right religion. Isaac sailed away again, this time to Rotterdam for a year of study. He acquired facility in the language that would be so important during his years in Canada.

At fifteen, Isaac received his first commission as an officer. His brother John had been promoted by purchase from lieutenant to captain. This left a vacancy in the 8th Regiment. His family was able to purchase an ensign's commission costing £400 for the next promising young soldier.

At that time a commission could be purchased for a lad under sixteen. In 1798, when Frederick Duke of York became the commander-in-chief of the army, he put a stop to commissions for boys too young to serve. No subaltern (ensign or lieutenant) could be commissioned until age sixteen. Some wealthy fathers would purchase commissions for sons as young as three or four years old. The boys would remain at school or in some such pastime until they turned sixteen, when they would take up their commissions. The value of early purchase was seniority. Once the name was placed in a regimental list, it moved up as vacancies occurred. For instance, where a commission had been allowed for a boy of six, he would enter the army ten years later and be eligible for a lieutenancy well ahead of boys who had waited until sixteen to be placed on the regimental list. Being less than a year underage, Isaac gained very little advantage from the purchase.

The practice of early purchase was grossly unfair. Promotions were assigned according to the ability to pay and seniority, not to competence or military experience. What is surprising is the number of first-quality officers the system did allow to reach the top commands. Isaac Brock was himself a fine example.

CHAPTER TWO

Ensign Brock

For the biographer, the years from 1785 to 1790 are obscure. Some information on the life of the 8th (or King's) Regiment of Foot yields clues, but there was a strange situation. Brock was an ensign, the lowliest commissioned rank, for five years. This was unusual. Most ensigns purchased lieutenancies within two years of joining their regiments. One who followed this pattern was Francis Simcoe, the eldest son of John Graves Simcoe, the first lieutenant-governor of Upper Canada (Ontario).

Francis's ensign's commission was signed at Whitehall, army headquarters, on October 30, 1807, when he was sixteen years, five months old. His lieutenant's commission was dated December 22, 1808, fourteen months later. What took Brock so long? Lack of money does not explain this. A lieutenancy cost £550, but the cost to Brock would be £150 because he would receive £400 from the sale of his ensign's commission.

He may not have felt ready for the greater responsibility of the higher rank. Although he was famous as an athlete, he realized that his general knowledge was inferior to that of his brother officers who had attended Eton or other great public schools that were better than his school at Southampton. He needed time to read, to study history and literature and political systems, to learn the military tactics and regimental administration that would be a necessary part of his work.

He was a competent horseman, a fair shot with a hunting rifle, and found that, after all his practice fencing with his fellow officers or his brothers, sword play came easily. The musket was another matter. It was inaccurate but quicker to load than a rifle and the best for war in the field. Soldiers in the ranks drilled for years before they could load, fire, and reload swiftly. A good infantryman had to be able to fire at least three shots a minute. They were trained to stand shoulder to shoulder in packed lines to stop an enemy advancing in like formation. Hours of drilling were devoted to learning to react automatically and quickly. Instead of a musket, an officer carried a pistol and a sword or sabre. However, if he wanted his men to respect him, he would have to be able to do anything he demanded of them.

Brock probably spent most of the summer of 1785 at home in St. Peter Port. He may also have paid a visit to the headquarters, or depot, of the 8th Regiment, which was in the northern English city of Liverpool. At that time the regiment was sailing home from Canada. It had been on duty there since 1768, and very active during the years of the American Revolution. Peace had come in 1784 by way of the Treaty of Paris, which gave the Thirteen Colonies their independence. The regiments no longer needed were returning, but that all took time. Fleets of ships, or transports, had to be assembled, and soldiers marched to ports of embarkation.

Returning with the 8th was Isaac's eldest brother, John. Although he had purchased his captaincy in the 8th, his name was not on the Army List for 1785, perhaps because he made changes after the list could be updated. On the list for 1801, John is shown as a captain in the 81st Regiment of Foot, dated July 8, 1795, and as brevet lieutenant colonel since January 1, 1798. "Brevet" meant that John was serving as the lieutenant colonel, but temporarily with a captain's rate of pay until the higher rank became available.

When Ensign Isaac Brock joined in 1785, the commander of the 8th Foot was Lieutenant Colonel Arent Schuyler De Peyster. While in North America, as well as his responsibility for the regiment, he had been commandant of Michilimackinac, then the fort at Detroit, and later at Fort Niagara. De Peyster was an American of Dutch-Belgian descent whose family had been in the colonies for several generations. By the 1760s they were part of the New York aristocracy. Arent's mother was a Schuyler, of an even more prominent "patroon" family. The Brock and De Peyster families had much in common. Both had bloodlines stretching back to non-British ancestors. De Peyster spoke Dutch, but he was an Anglican and an anglophile with the air of an English gentleman. The Brocks belonged to Guernsey, and knew the patois. English was their natural language and they saw themselves as English patriots.

If John Brock's changes in rank were too rapid for the annual printings of the Army List, the same may be said for Isaac's. Other sources state that in 1790 he sold his ensign's commission in the 8th Regiment for £400 and purchased a lieutenancy, valued at £550, but this is not shown on the list. Brock had to raise only £150 to cover the difference between the two commissions.

The commissioned officer's uniform for the 8th Regiment was a scarlet coat, faced blue. His gorget, half-moon shaped and worn suspended by a ribbon on his chest, was of gold, as were his buttons and the lacing on his black-cocked felt hat. His breeches and waistcoat were white. The officer's sash worn around his waist was of deep red silk.

Isaac was already working towards his captaincy, as commander of a company. The price for an established regiment would be £1,500, a very great sum at the time. One reason it was so much more expensive than ensign or lieutenant was that not as many captaincies were required. With so few places available, the army was able to demand the much higher price.

A regiment of foot consisted of ten companies, usually of fifty to one hundred private men, governed by one or two sergeants and three corporals. Young boys served as drummers and fifers to beat and pipe the signals. Eight companies, known as battalion companies, formed the middle of the battalion. In front marched the light company, whose uniforms and accoutrements were less heavy so that they could move more rapidly. To the rear was the grenadier company, as far as possible composed of men at least six feet tall, clad in tall bearskin caps to make them appear even more intimidating. When drawn up in line of battle the light company stood on the left, to serve as skirmishers, while the grenadiers stood on the right to give extra strength to the push.

By 1790 Isaac knew that there was a way other than purchase to gain a captaincy. When the government authorized the raising of some new independent companies, he seized the opportunity. The Army List for 1791 shows Isaac Brock as the captain of an independent company. Listed as his ensign was Isaac's youngest brother,

Irving Brock, now aged sixteen. Commissions were handed out after an applicant had raised the desired number of recruits. Once the company was at strength, Isaac had earned his captaincy and Irving his ensigncy. Isaac had raised most of his recruits in Guernsey and Jersey.

For recruiting he had received a "beating warrant," which gave him permission to go through the countryside accompanied by a drummer beating to attract attention. Actually, a commissioned officer, therefore a gentleman, rarely soiled his hands by recruiting in person; a sergeant, a non-commissioned officer (NCO), would accompany the drummer to harangue the young men who gathered, to persuade them that nothing could be more noble than a career in His Majesty's army. The recruiters, naturally, overlooked the nastier side of army life, including low pay with stoppages for lost or replaced equipment and medical care. These items took most of the pay of one shilling per day. Nor did recruiters dwell on horrendous floggings for minor breaches of the rules or execution by firing squad of deserters who were apprehended.

The British army was being kept close to full strength because of worry over events in France. Ironically, France had helped the Americans against the British during their revolution. Now the French were following their example. Yet independence had brought problems of administration to the infant United States. The new country was encumbered with debts from the long war. Throughout the 1790s power struggles within France had been leading to changes in leadership and finally to the rise of a young Corsican named Napoleon Bonaparte with ambitions for world domination. (Bonaparte, the Duke of Wellington who deposed him, and Isaac Brock were all born in the same year.)

The French Revolution brought an influx of new people to Guernsey and the other Channel Islands. French *emigrés* who escaped the abolition of Christianity were making their way to the islands in search of security. Before the migration of new French blood, there were ten Anglican parishes on Guernsey. To these, over several years, were added three Roman Catholic parishes. Others who made inroads were Methodists, who were visited in 1787 by the aged John Wesley himself. In neither case were the new denominations welcomed at first. Crowds sometimes gathered to jeer at missionaries of Rome, and outdoor Methodist meetings ended in disorder.

Meanwhile, Isaac Brock became dissatisfied with his independent company. Too many had been raised, and these were serving as garrisons close to home. In fact, Isaac and Irving and several other officers had been placed on half-pay. Disillusioned, young Irving resigned his commission. His brother William, now twenty-seven, had become a partner in a bank. Irving began an apprenticeship under William's guidance.

William's success solved Isaac's problems over the direction his future should take. He was able to transfer from a half-pay captain of an independent company to a company in the 49th Regiment of Foot, as of June 15, 1791. The cost of his captaincy in an established regiment would have been £950 in addition to the £550 he received for the sale of his lieutenancy. One source suggests that he "exchanged" (traded up with no money involved), another that he paid the difference in order to exchange into the 49th. What is not clear is whether the difference was £950 or some lesser amount.

Whichever way, William was able to finance further promotions by purchase. Captain Isaac Brock's rise in the army now became spectacularly rapid.

CHAPTER THREE

The Regiment, 1791–1798

Captain Isaac Brock of the 49th was twenty-one years, nine months when his commission was signed on June 15, 1791. He had a tailor change the facings on his coat from the blue of the 8th to green. The gorget and other accoutrements remained gold; the lace trim around the rows of buttons and button-holes was white with two red and one green stripe. Breeches and waistcoat remained white, although fatigues — trousers of grey or dark blue — were being assigned to the men in the ranks as more practical for daily work. As in his time as ensign and lieutenant, Isaac wore a single epaulette of gold thread on his left shoulder. The 49th would be the regiment identified with Brock for the rest of his career.

According to the Army List for 1790, the colonel of the 49th was the Hon. Alexander Maitland, who was also a lieutenant general in the army. The lieutenant colonel, James Grant, was the commander of the battalion. Colonel of a regiment was usually an honorary title given to some respected officer who also held a higher rank.

Isaac's promotion in the 49th meant his expenses were greater; he now needed a servant and had higher mess bills. William's generosity took care of these necessities. For his servant Brock hired a man he referred to only as Dobson, who was with him throughout most of his military career. Dobson would nurse him through a bout of fever in the West Indies, but would predecease him by a few months.

As the 49th was stationed in Barbados, the ocean voyage was next on Isaac's agenda. For the moment he would not need a horse. He might have to purchase one when he reached the regiment, but he suspected that horses did not do well in the subtropical heat. He was pleased and proud as he set out. At last he ought to be doing more satisfying work, and in an established regiment with, he assumed, a fine reputation.

Upon arriving, he felt like a new boy at school. He had to endure teasing and rowdiness from his brother officers, which he took with aplomb. The best stories are preserved in a biography compiled by his nephew, Ferdinand Brock Tupper, a son of Isaac's sister Elizabeth. From Tupper comes the tale about a duel.

An arrogant, rather small-sized officer who was known as a "professional duellist" and a crack shot challenged Brock on a trumped-up excuse. He expected an easy conquest because Brock, being large, made a target that would be almost impossible to miss. The weapons would be pistols. Brock accepted the challenge to the duel, but only if, instead of marching back to back and at twelve paces, the customary range before turning and firing, they each fire across a handkerchief — in other words, at point blank range! The other backed down, to the delight and derision of the officers. The would-be duellist was so dishonoured that he had no choice but to resign from the regiment. Duelling was forbidden, but that did not stop the settling of scores by secret dawn meetings. Accompanied by their seconds, who made the arrangements and chose a secluded spot, they brought along a surgeon to patch up the loser.

Brock was a newcomer to the regiment, and as yet an untried captain. Owing to other incidents of quick thinking, he was soon making his mark as a reliable leader, one who had good judgement. Junior officers, NCOs, and the private men in the ranks would have no hesitation in following where he led.

Barbados was not a healthy place to be on duty. The subtropical islands of the Caribbean were infamous for fevers. Losses through disease and death were heavy, which made the posting unpopular. Little is known about how the men passed their time. Brock took long swims, less for enjoyment or to prove himself than for coolness. Slackness was not tolerated. Too many neighbouring islands belonged to France, too close for comfort. The men required some drilling, but everyone was apathetic in the debilitating heat. The garrison had to be constantly watching lest an attacking force appear offshore.

Another depressing aspect to Barbados was that a scarcity of young women interfered with regimental social life. At dances, officers found themselves steering ladies old enough to be their mothers, or standing on the sidelines because there were never enough white women of any age on the island.

After a few months, the regiment moved to Jamaica, which Brock found to be a small improvement. There were more young women to charm the officers, but that did not make this island a happier place. On both Barbados and Jamaica, the economy was based on sugar. On huge plantations long stocks of sugar cane waved in the breeze, and all work was performed by black slaves. Back in England, led by William Wilberforce, an abolitionist movement was growing. John Graves Simcoe, now in Upper Canada, tried to abolish slavery outright, but his legislative council would not support him. He had to settle for phasing it out. Children born to slaves would be free at age twenty-five, and their children free from birth. Slaves in Upper Canada were few in number. In Jamaica, where the black workers far outnumbered the white dwellers, people lived in constant fear of a slave uprising.

Jamaica was 467 kilometres (280 miles) further north, and slightly more comfortable. Still the fevers persisted, and the number of men fit for duty declined. Even for men accustomed to the milder climate of Guernsey and the other Channel Islands, the heat was oppressive. Men from cool rainy England, especially those from the north and Scotsmen, suffered cruelly.

On nearby Hispanola (now Haiti and the Dominican Republic), there had been an uprising following the over-throw of the royalists in France. While colonists were allowed representation in the French National Assembly, former slaves were not. The French royalists of the half of the island known as San Domingo were asking the British governor of Jamaica, Adam Williamson, for help against the anti-slavery republicans. They wanted Williamson to supply British troops to restore order. The matter was still under discussion in 1793 when, despite his rugged constitution, Isaac Brock became ill. His servant, Dobson, cared for him, but because he took too long to become well, he applied for a leave of absence.

At the same time, a force of one thousand British troops landed at Port au Prince, San Domingo. More than half of them were dead of yellow fever and malaria within six weeks. Such was the hazard of service in the dangerous islands. Between 1793 and 1796, the British lost seventy-five hundred men to fever and malaria. Some were from companies of Brock's own 49th. In May 1796, a further seven thousand landed on San Domingo, by which time the 49th Regiment was on its way home. In January 1797, Lieutenant General John Graves Simcoe, the abolitionist, was at home on leave from governing Upper Canada. Ironically, Simcoe was chosen as commandant and civil governor of San Domingo. The mutual hatred between slave and master was so brutal that Simcoe ordered cruelties and outrages to cease, but with little effect. By August, ill and angry, Simcoe was back in England. He was the last British governor to try to rule San Domingo.

After Brock had recuperated at home in St. Peter Port, he took up recruiting again, sometimes in Guernsey, more often in Jersey. Tension still ran high. No one knew what France might do next. Stationed on Jersey and Guernsey were fencible corps, raised for service at home. Brock became acquainted with a man who would serve him a few years later in the Canadas.

He was the Reverend Alexander Macdonell, a Roman Catholic priest and the chaplain of the First Glengarry Fencible Corps. This regiment had been raised among Highlanders of Glengarry, Scotland, through the influence of Macdonell. He wanted employment for the many starving tenant farmers whose landlords had evicted them in what were known as the

"Highland Clearances." The owners wanted to raise sheep on their lands because sheep were more profitable than people. The Gaelic-speaking Highlanders, many named Macdonell, were excellent troops. Their chaplain was destined to become the Bishop of Regiopolis, the first Roman Catholic diocese in Upper Canada.

By 1795 Brock was able to purchase a major's commission in the 49th, for £2,000. This made him equal to his eldest brother, John, who was stationed in Cape Town, South Africa, and now a major in the 81st Regiment. Isaac needed £500 to buy the commission once he had sold his captaincy for £1,500. Again William helped him. His battalion in the 49th required two majors. Each would lead a wing, or five companies, if the regiment went to war or if it was to be divided and stationed in two different places. Brock became the senior major on June 24, 1795; the junior major, appointed on September 1, was John Vincent, a name that would appear often in the records of the 49th in Upper Canada.

During the year 1795, Isaac's mother, Elizabeth, died. Losing someone special was always a blow, but Brock was comforted that he had not been off in some far corner of the world during her last days. His eldest sister, Elizabeth, and her husband, John Tupper, moved into the family house in the centre of St. Peter Port. One of their sons was Ferdinand Brock Tupper, the author of the most important source on Isaac's life in the army.

Although Brock was now a proud senior major in the 49th, he had maintained some contact with officers of the 8th. The year of his majority, Lieutenant Colonel Arent De Peyster retired. He left Liverpool for Dumfries, in Galloway, Scotland, to Mavis Grove, the house his wife had inherited from her family. Long a writer of poems to amuse himself, he soon found a kindred spirit in a young excise man responsible for keeping home-distilled whiskey off the market.

Because of the danger from France, De Peyster took command of the Dumfries Volunteer Corps. Serving in the corps was the bard, already renowned, poet and Scottish national treasure, Robert (Robbie) Burns.

Their backgrounds could not have been more different — one a colonial aristocrat, the other a poor farm boy, but one whose thirst for knowledge had elevated him to one of the best-loved sons of Scotland. The two friends exchanged poems. Published in the complete works of Burns is the "Poem on Life. Addressed to Colonel De Peyster, Dumfries, 1796."

The words are in a dialect called Broad Scots. Part of it reads:

> O what a canty warld were it,
> Would pain and care, and sickness spare it:
> And fortune favor worth and merit,
> As they deserve:

(And aye a rowth, roast beef and claret:
And wha would starve?)

Burns was a dying man. The end came in 1797 at the age of just thirty-seven. De Peyster passed on in 1822 at age eighty-six. His grave lies next to Burns's, two friends in life, companions still in death.

Creating poems and holding readings was a popular pastime among officers serving abroad as well as on their home turf. Nothing found suggests that Brock wrote poetry, but poems to Brock were written, and at least two were set to music. The papers of John Graves Simcoe show that he and his military friends wrote many poems, most of Simcoe's best forgotten.

When the 49th was sent home from the West Indies in July 1796, Brock and his fellow officers had their hands full working to improve the condition of the regiment and its members. The ranks had been depleted by the time spent in the Caribbean. Recruits had to be found to bring the corps up to full strength with ten companies, each of fifty privates, plus NCOs and new officers. The clothing was worn out, equipment needed repair and replacement, and new recruits had to be drilled. By now Brock was not satisfied to serve as a subordinate; he wanted to have sole command.

The only way he could succeed was to purchase the lieutenant colonelcy when it became available, which would cost £3,500. This meant another £1,500 after the sale of his major's commission. William again backed him for the commission and for his other needs: extra servants, a good horse, and a headquarters. William did not expect Isaac to reimburse him. His brother was an investment, and William had faith in him.

His commission as the junior lieutenant colonel in the 49th was signed on October 25, 1797, not quite three weeks after his twenty-eighth birthday. However, he was one step away from taking command of the battalion. Less than thirteen years had passed since he was first commissioned, a fine record, but he still had to answer to the senior lieutenant colonel, Frederick Keppel. For the moment, Isaac would not have the command of a battalion, nor was he ready for so much responsibility. He had moved rapidly upward, but he had not had any battle experience, which was a decided disadvantage. One could say that he had never seen a shot fired in anger.

A year later, in 1798, Keppel resigned, and Brock became the senior lieutenant colonel of a greatly expanded and improved 49th. His second youngest brother, Savery, now joined him as the regimental paymaster. Savery's appointment was dated February 15, 1798. Isaac's junior lieutenant colonel was a man nearly six years older. He had been commissioned ensign at age fifteen, in 1787, although like Brock he did not have battle experience. His name was Roger Hale Sheaffe.

CHAPTER FOUR

1799 Holland–1801 Copenhagen

B rock was now preparing in earnest for his first real fight. During the many struggles against France, alliances formed, broke apart, re-formed with the same friends, or with others who had changed sides. By 1799, Napoleon had become first consul of France and was rising spectacularly, while Britain, Austria, Russia, Holland, Naples, Portugal, and others sought to restrain the armies of revolutionary France. The French were learning to fight in a new style, in which full battalions heavily packed together were able to destroy the traditional lines of many continental European armies.

Holland

The first opportunity for Brock and his revitalized 49th Foot came in the summer of 1799. The mission was to assist the Dutch in northwest Holland, where a French army had overrun the countryside. The British expedition was under the command of General Sir Ralph Abercromby, of the prominent military family. The 49th was part of the advance brigade led by Major General John Moore (later Sir John, who died near Corunna, Spain, in 1809).

On August 27, Moore's advance brigade landed at Den Holder, a strong position beside what today is the North Holland Canal, six miles from the North Sea, at an opening into the Zuiderzee. The rest of Abercromby's force soon caught up. The expedition set off southward, making for Alkmaar, some thirty miles off. They marched along the dune belt that protected the low-lying drained farmlands from the sea. They met little opposition until September 10, when they halted upon spotting French battalions drawn up along the flanks. The enemy was under the command of Guillame Marie Anne Brune, marshal of the French Empire.

Swinging from line of march to line of battle, the closely packed troops had enough firepower to beat off the French battalions. Dispersing the close battalion formation proved to be not too difficult. Once the British muskets had mowed down the first soldiers who approached, the more rearward lines were plunged into confusion as those behind sought to advance through piles of dead and wounded.

The 49th stood by in the reserve, Brock's drummers ready to give the signal as soon as he received the order to advance. None came. The French were driven off without their participation — a disappointment. Moore may have kept the young 49th out of the action deliberately. Both their commanding lieutenant colonel and the rank and file were "green." Moore believed firmly in training and more training, as much as possible not letting them get blood-ied too soon. At that point, Brock, too, admitted the necessity of a well-trained, well-disciplined battalion, probably because he saw how right Moore was.

On September 13, Prince Frederick the Duke of York arrived — he had been the commander-in-chief since April 3, 1798. He led a fleet of transports bringing reinforcements. From the east the army received a fur-ther reinforcement of Russians. On October 2, they fought an action that was commemorated on the colours of the British regiments that took part as "Egmont-op-Zee" (more correctly Egmond ann Zee). This time Marshal Brune was better prepared, and this time Moore allowed the 49th to join the front line of battle.

The 49th, being heavily engaged, acquitted itself well. Brock was proud, but not entirely clear on how they had won praise. The battle, fought among the sand dunes and waving grasses, was disjointed. The lieutenant colonel himself was "slightly wounded" by a spent ball, one that had lost momentum by the time it struck him. In a letter to his brother John he wrote: "I got knocked down short-ly after the enemy began to retreat, but never quitted the field, and returned to my duty in less than half an hour."

What he kept to himself for the moment was how he was saved from serious injury, or worse. The day was very cold. He had wrapped several cravats (large silk ties) around his throat. While unwinding them he found a ball that gave him a bruise but did not pene-trate through all the layers of cloth. In this first real bat-tle, thirty-three men of the 49th were killed outright or died of wounds soon afterward. Brock was horrified by such a great loss. For the first time, but not the last, he wondered whether acting less boldly might have spared more of his men. Other officers in the brigade reassured him. Considering the weight of the struggle, his men had come off lightly.

The allies — British, Russian, and Dutch — occu-pied Egmond, inland from Egmond ann Zee, and the substantial trading centre on drained lands. When the French attacked, the allies were badly mauled, but not the 49th, for it was again held in reserve. Some officers whispered that Moore had thought Brock somewhat too bold in the earlier action.

The Duke of York was alarmed by the force of the French attack. He asked for a "convention," or agreement, allowing his army to embark for England without interference. The French agreed, and the campaign ended having failed to protect the Dutch. By the Convention of Alkmaar, signed on October 18, Holland was secured for France.

The regiment, and the Russian allies, moved to quarters in Jersey. Brock took the opportunity to visit his family on Guernsey for a few days. On his return to the regiment he found out, for first time, that his subordinate, Lieutenant Colonel Sheaffe, was not at all popular with the men of the 49th. With Brock back in charge, the cheerful atmosphere he inspired returned.

Sheaffe had served as an officer in the 5th Regiment at Fort Niagara, where he was promoted to captain. He'd had a good relationship with Governor Simcoe, who described him as "incapable of any intemperate or uncivil conduct." Simcoe was a close friend of the honorary colonel of the 5th, Hugh Percy, the second Duke of Northumberland, who was Sheaffe's benefactor. Northumberland had come to know the Sheaffe family while stationed in Boston during the American Revolution. He resided in the boarding house kept by Sheaffe's widowed mother, Susannah, where he took a fancy to her young son. Northumberland sent him to a military academy in

Chelsea, near London, and paid for his protegé's commissions in the army.

Sheaffe seems to have worked out well until he came under Brock. Being five years older than his senior lieutenant colonel may have left him feeling jealous. Others have suggested that he was teased about being an American, and not well born. Another explanation was that Sheaffe was a sadist who enjoyed bullying his inferiors. One who criticized him often in his memoirs was James FitzGibbon, a well-known personality in nineteenth-century York.

FitzGibbon was a lowly Irish lad of nineteen when he joined the 49th. He was born at Glin, Ireland, in 1780, the son of a weaver and also a tenant farmer of the Knight of Glin. He had received little education. He joined Glin's Yeomanry Corps, where he was promoted sergeant. In 1798 he joined a fencible regiment. Fencibles, raised for duty at home, were not expected to go abroad. FitzGibbon was next recruited into the 49th, which would give him opportunities to become a professional soldier. He was with the regiment in Holland, where he was again promoted sergeant.

Copenhagen

In April 1801, Prime Minister William Pitt (the younger) authorized an expedition against Denmark. The Danes were attempting to close the Elbe River to the Germans, at the time valued allies of Britain. To intimidate the Danes, an expedition commanded by Admiral Sir Hyde Parker sailed to the Baltic Sea. The second in command was Vice Admiral Horatio Nelson, who would prove himself one of the greatest naval men at the Battle of Trafalgar. The senior army officer was Lieutenant Colonel William Stewart of the rifle corps.

Because this was primarily a naval exercise, Brock's 49th was one of the few regiments involved, and the men were distributed on various ships. James FitzGibbon was one of the 49th who served as marines. The job of the red-coated marines was to keep order aboard the ship. The fleet consisted of twenty ships of the line and some smaller frigates.

The route for the fleet was a long one. The ships had to sail to the north of the northernmost part of mainland Denmark, through the Scagerrak passage, then south through the Kattegat, between the Swedish west coast below Goteborg and the island of Zealand. Copenhagen, the Danish capital, lay on the east side of Zealand, with part of the city on the small island of Amager, which helped form the sheltered harbour.

James FitzGibbon recorded that the 49th left Jersey for Portsmouth, and on to Horsham, Sussex, where they expected to stay for some time. Then an order came from the Horse Guards for their immediate return to Portsmouth, but instead they were to be embarked at Spithead on board a man-of-war to serve as marines. At first the grenadiers were aboard Nelson's flagship, the *St. George*. The ships at Spithead that were intended for the Baltic sailed to Yarmouth, and there the grenadiers were transferred to the much smaller *Monarch*. The fleet sailed on March 12 and anchored below Elsinore on March 29. Nelson ordered that not a shot was to be fired from his guns, but some shots from the *Monarch* damaged the walls of the castle of Elsinore.

The plan was to attack Copenhagen by soldiers and some blue-jacketed sailors. The Danes were ready for them. They had built gun batteries on piles in the harbour, dangerous for the attacking expedition, ready to exact a high cost in lives. The Danes had ten battleships of the line and the deadly batteries. While Parker stayed in reserve, Nelson attacked with twelve ships. When three of them ran aground, he proceeded with only nine, which the Danes greeted with punishing resistance. Worried that Nelson was too weak, Parker hoisted a signal flag for all ships to retire. Now occurred the legendary incident where Nelson put his telescope to his blind eye and called, "I see no flag!" Ignoring Parker, he continued sailing towards the enemy.

He attacked many Danish craft moored off Copenhagen, until April 2 when the Danish fire ceased. The British had lost twelve hundred men, with six ships heavily damaged. The Danes had lost one ship sunk, and the rest were so badly damaged that they were helpless.

During the struggle in the harbour of Copenhagen, Brock was aboard the ship *Ganges* with some of his men. When the battle came to an end he was rowed to Nelson's flagship, now the *Elephant,* for a visit and the opportunity to meet with the brilliant admiral in person.

In what had been a bloody engagement, the 49th suffered thirteen killed and forty-one wounded. For a naval battle where their participation was small, the losses were great. Afterwards the regiment again returned to Jersey, where training and recruiting continued. Brock may have made a call on his family, but more likely he remained with his men, rather than trust them again to the mercies of Lieutenant Colonel Sheaffe.

After one land battle where the 49th spent more time in reserve than in the line, and one that was mainly a naval battle, the regiment was still very "young." One American, retired Colonel David Fitz-Enz, writing in 2001, described Brock as "an experienced professional officer who had fought in India and in numerous engagements throughout the empire."

A quick glance at more than one dictionary of biography, or a book of military history, might have put him straight. What did Fitz-Enz hope to achieve by reinventing Isaac Brock? Did he have to make Brock appear a seasoned veteran? More likely he was making excuses for the poor performances of generals who were aged leftovers from the American Revolution. Or perhaps he was making excuses for incompetence of men who received important appointments through the help of friends among the politicians.

PART II

Canada

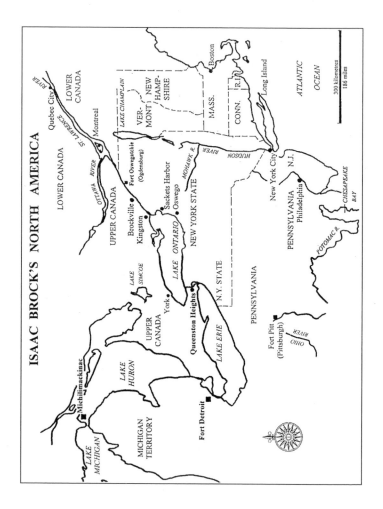

ISAAC BROCK'S NORTH AMERICA

CHAPTER FIVE

First Posting to the Canadas

In the summer of 1801, the 49th Regiment moved from Jersey to Colchester, and then in the autumn to Chelmsford. There, James FitzGibbon recalled, the men passed the winter in comfort, but with a rigorous program of training. During the stay at Chelmsford, FitzGibbon found himself in an awkward predicament. Before it was over he had learned what a sensible, fair-minded commander Isaac Brock was.

At the time, FitzGibbon was the pay sergeant of the grenadier company. Owing to a weak grounding in arithmetic, he found that he had lost track of two pounds. He was both horrified and terrified. The discovery of this loss would lead to a charge of theft, demotion to private in the ranks, a hearing, and a flogging. He pictured the regiment drawn up in the parade square, himself marched out stripped to the waist, tied to the triangle, and sentenced to many strokes of the lash. Influenced, he claimed, by his early reading of historical romances, FitzGibbon decided to appeal to the commander-in-chief for protection:

> I asked for and obtained a pass for three days to go to London on pretended business. I walked up the town and found my way to the Anchor and Vines tavern, close to the Horse Guards and, though tired, at once wrote a letter to the Duke of York, stating the case to him and praying of him to enable me to replace the money so that my colonel might not know of the deficiency; for, as I looked upon him as the father of the regiment, I dreaded the forfeiture of his good opinion more than any other consequence which might follow.[1]

The following morning he gave his letter in at the door of the Horse Guards. This, the military building in the Whitehall complex, housed the commander-in-chief and his staff. FitzGibbon walked back and forth until

1. In the 1890s, Mary Agnes FitzGibbon collected the letters and memoirs of her grandfather and published them as *A Veteran of 1812: The Life and Times of James FitzGibbon*. The quotations in this chapter are from this collection. Background also incorporated was supplied by Mary Agnes. Both materials were taken from the opening pages of Chapter 4.

nightfall when he returned to the tavern. Then, fearing
that his letter might not be given to the Duke, he wrote
a second letter, which he took to the door at the Horse
Guards before opening time. He asked a sentry to point
out the Duke to him. The other did, a happy co-operation because FitzGibbon did not recognize him in his
civilian dress. The Duke took the letter and passed on
without speaking. FitzGibbon continued:

> After a lapse of a few, to me most anxious
> minutes, I was called, shown into a wait-
> ing-room upstairs and told that Colonel
> Brownrigg would see me. He came in
> presently with my two letters in his hand.
> He asked me if I had written them. I
> answered, "Yes." Upon which he said,
> "The Duke can do nothing in this matter
> before referring to your colonel."
>
> "But it is to avoid that I have made
> this application."
>
> "The Duke is not displeased with
> you," Brownrigg replied. "Return to
> your regiment and you will not be
> treated harshly."

As it was now too late to reach Chelmsford that
night, he returned to the tavern. Having never been to

a theatre before, he went to Drury Lane, and learning that he could sit in the gallery for half price he went in and watched a play. When he awoke on the final morning of his leave, he felt feverish. He wrote a note to the regiment's London agents reporting his illness and asking them to forward the note to Chelmsford explaining why he would be overdue. In the afternoon a servant came to his room and announced that two gentlemen were downstairs and asking to see him. He asked them to be shown up, and to his dismay in walked Colonel Brock and another officer of the 49th.

"Well, young man, what's the matter with you?" Brock began.

"A cold, Colonel," FitzGibbon replied.

"Well," he said. "Take care of yourself this night and return to the regiment tomorrow. Perhaps your money is all spent." He laid a half guinea on the table beside him with the words, "That is enough to take you home."

"If you knew what brought me here, you would not be so kind to me."

"I know all about it. Get well and go back to the regiment."

The colonel had come up to London that morning, and was at the agents' when FitzGibbon's note arrived. He then went to the Duke of York's office, where the two letters were handed over, after which he paid his visit to the tavern. Later in the evening the colonel's servant, Dobson, came. He was a private servant, not a soldier, and, FitzGibbon thought, very intelligent.

"What's this that you've been doing at the Horse Guards?" Dobson began.

"What I would gladly conceal from the world."

"Well, I know something about it, for while attending at table at the colonel's brother's house today, I overheard a good deal of what the colonel said of you to the company. It seems you have been writing letters to the Duke of York about some difficulty you have got yourself into, and mentioned the colonel in a way that pleased him and his brother. When the Duke gave him your letters he recommended you to him, saying that His Grace would not forget FitzGibbon. Then the colonel added, 'If the Duke forgets him I will not.'"

The brother with the London house was William, the banker, and also a merchant. The bank in Guernsey was affiliated with a major London one, which required William to have a home away from home to conduct his business.

Back in Chelmsford, FitzGibbon's accounts were examined by a junior officer, who found an error of one pound, fifteen shillings. That and a second of five shillings accounted for all the missing funds. The rest of the winter and the spring of 1802 were taken up in constant drilling, using as a guide a new code written by General John Moore, for which Moore was becoming famous.

After more recruiting, the 49th was ready for strenuous duty. Brock was informed that his regiment would be embarking shortly for Quebec, on a voyage that might last two months. How Brock felt about this order is not known, but by 1802 the wars of the French Revolution (1789–1798) had become the Napoleonic Wars. Canada was a backwater that needed to be protected against the expansionist notions of the young United States of America. Opportunities for winning fame and promotions would be restricted there. Far better was a career against Napoleon's battalions.

The 49th embarked in June, arriving at Quebec in late August. Encouraged by Brock, James FitzGibbon used the less demanding time at sea to advantage by studying books on military tactics, spelling, and arithmetic. He memorized the "Rules and Regulations for the Field Exercises of His Majesty's Forces." Brock was passing the time reading the classics or works of history, improving his own education after his athletic but not very intellectual youth.

As far as Brock knew when they landed, the 49th was to be sent to the frontier posts in what was called the Upper Country. Until Jay's Treaty, which limited arms on the Great Lakes, had been ratified, the forts at Michilimackinac, Detroit, Fort Niagara, and smaller posts had been held by the British. Following the treaty, the British garrisons were withdrawn and replaced by

American troops. A new line of forts was then constructed to protect Canadian territory.

From a fort on St. Joseph's Island, the garrison could keep watch on the American garrison at Michilimackinac; Fort Malden was built near Amherstburg as a counterweight to the fort at Detroit; Fort George, at Newark (Niagara-on-the-Lake), served the same purpose near Fort Niagara; and the Kingston garrison kept watch on Oswego. Military headquarters were at York, the tiny capital named by Governor Simcoe in honour of a victory at Famars by the Duke of York. (In August 1793, the Duke's army had driven the French out of Holland. The naming of York was a trifle premature. In a counterattack some weeks later, the French drove the Duke's force back, turning the earlier victory into a rout.)

The plan to send the regiment west was altered. Instead the 49th would spend the winter of 1802–03 in Montreal. A fleet of bateaux was gathered at wharves along the waterfront of the Lower Town. Anyone familiar with August in the St. Lawrence Valley would sympathize with the men of the 49th, and the women and children travelling with them. The heat and the high humidity were almost as miserable as the climate of the Caribbean. The heavy regulation clothing added to the misery. During training on the Champ de Mars, reserved as a parade ground, the sight of a soldier lying prostrate was part of the scenery.

The Champ de Mars, which lay north of the present St. James Street, west of the fort, was the focal point for the city. There the fashionable would promenade in front of the courthouse, to see and be seen. Regimental bands often played for the crowd in the evenings. The open space allowed plenty of room for crowds who flocked to view public executions. Further west on Notre Dame Street was the jail, not far off. Parents brought their children to watch the hangings, as a warning for them to behave or one day they might share the fate of the wretch dangling at the end of the rope.

For a long overseas posting, each company was permitted to have five soldiers' wives accompany it, and those with children were allowed to bring them. The wives were there as housekeepers. The women and children led miserable lives, sleeping wherever they could find a space in the barracks. Yet they were better off than wives and children who were left behind, without husbands and fathers to provide for them.

Montreal, Brock discovered, had at least six thousand residents. The old part of the city was surrounded by a wall, now dilapidated. The part inside the wall was about one hundred acres, which was the extent of the French city when British troops captured it in 1760. Now houses were spreading well beyond the wall. A onetime nunnery within the walled part had been converted into a large barracks, but many smaller buildings beyond the walls were also used as barracks.

The old fort at the eastern end of the wall was also much dilapidated. Brock, being Brock, at once set about improving the wall and rebuilding the fort. The men worked in grey linen trousers and their shirtsleeves; the heavy wool jackets, described as brick red, were left in their barracks. The work on the defences was of utmost importance. Brock could see that Montreal was too close to the United States border, facing an easy route north from Lake Champlain.

The view to the north of Montreal was spectacular. Beyond the St. Lawrence plain rose the forested Monteregian Hills. In the foreground were many orchards where very fine apples grew. Although still smaller than Quebec, which had about eight thousand residents, Montreal was becoming the commercial heart of the Canadas. The headquarters and banking offices of the Northwest Fur Trading Company dominated the economy. Set up to divert trade from the Hudson's Bay Company, the Nor'westers' canoes penetrated the posts across the west, bringing wealth to the city.

With the wealth came tensions between the French-speaking residents and the more recent English business interests. The French elite owned the *seigneuries*, where the land was worked by tenants, or *habitants*. Unlike the other members of the British Empire, Roman Catholics had the same civil rights as they had held under the

French regime. The newcomers, and the government of English-speaking officers, looked upon the older residents as a conquered people. In truth, they were not so much conquered as abandoned by France, who valued islands in the Caribbean over the *arpents de niege*.

For the officers and men of the 49th, autumn brought welcome relief from the heat, until in November the intense cold began. Now Brock had to ensure that the regiment had a good stock of firewood and blankets. The men were employed in blocking up cracks in the many wooden buildings. By Christmas some of the Scottish Highland soldiers were wearing trousers underneath their kilts to protect their knees from frostbite.

For Brock the winter passed pleasantly. He found that winter was the time for friendships. Comfortable in English and French, he made friends with both groups. The French *seigneurs* resembled the elite of Guernsey. He did not mix with the traders and merchant class, but he spent happy times with senior officers. Some of the luckier ones had brought their wives, which made visits to homes so enjoyable. Balls were frequent, with many opportunities for dancing and good company. Despite the cold, travel was easy by sleigh over packed snow roads or on the frozen rivers. His one dismay was the length of the cold time.

By March, Brock found no hint of spring. He dreamed of the wealth of flowers on Guernsey, and even in England, but in Montreal the temperatures continued to be frigid. Orders soon came for the 49th to move on to Upper Canada once the ice left the St. Lawrence. Headquarters would still be in the capital, York, with troops also stationed at Fort George, at the foot of the Niagara River. In the midst of his preparations, Brock received unwelcome news from home.

His eldest brother, John, still serving as a major in the 81st Regiment at Cape Town, was dead. He had been supervising a regimental ball where one of his brother officers appeared with a woman not acceptable in polite company. When John ordered the officer, revealed only as Capt. M———, to remove her, he found himself challenged to a duel. Unlike Isaac, John apparently could not call the other's bluff. The duellist's shot struck home, ending John's life at age forty-three. To Isaac, John's death seemed a terrible waste of an active, useful life.

Of the family of fourteen, now only eight were alive. Savery had resigned as the regimental paymaster and had gone to England, intending to work as a reporter in the struggles with the French. His replacement as paymaster was a cousin, James Brock. Back home, his brother Daniel had recently been elected a jurat of the Royal Court of Guernsey. Irving, the youngest, now twenty-seven, was having success as a banker, assisting William, who had recently married. Some of Isaac's letters from the Canadas were addressed to Mrs. William Brock; they seemed to be kindred spirits.

CHAPTER SIX

Desertions and Mutiny, 1802–04

In the spring of 1803, Brock and the 49th began the journey to York. They would be travelling in brigades of bateaux because so much of the St. Lawrence west of Montreal was a struggle against stretches of rapids, a stiff current, and the prevailing southwest wind. For ships of deeper draft, the head of navigation was below the Lachine Rapids. The regiment marched to Lachine. (Jokers who named the place insisted that here was the only China the great LaSalle would ever find in his quest for a northwest passage to China's riches across North America.)

On rare days when the wind was from the northeast, a lateen sail could carry the bateau comfortably, but too often the crews, assisted by soldiers, had to row. Many bateaux were required to hold some five hundred men, with the more spacious ones reserved for the officers and

The Archives of Ontario, John Ross Robertson Collection.

Mrs. Elizabeth Simcoe's watercolour sketch of Burlington Bay, 1790s. The scene was a familiar sight for General Brock, 1804 and 1810–12.

their vast quantity of baggage. They passed through Lake St. Louis and the Lake of Two Mountains, which led to the mouth of the Ottawa River. A shallow canal dug during the American Revolution bypassed the Cedars and Cascade Rapids.

Along the St. Lawrence they passed the little settlements of American Loyalists who had settled there from 1784 onwards. Most husbands and fathers had served in Provincial Corps of the British army — Loyalist regiments. People were working hard on their farms, but what made the strongest impression on Brock and the others was the dark, enclosing forest.

The first township west of the last French *seigneury* had been left empty until 1785, when Gaelic-speaking

Scots Highlanders came to settle. As many were Roman Catholics, the government thought they would not cause friction with their French-speaking neighbours. The mainly Protestant Loyalists were further west in the Royal Townships, so called because they had been named after the many children of King George III.

The Highlanders were especially interesting to Brock. He had held them in favour when he encountered the First Glengarry Fencible Corps and their chaplain, Father Macdonell, when they were on duty in Guernsey and Jersey. Brock had very few regular soldiers in Upper Canada. The Highlanders would make fine recruits for the militia (citizen soldiers who were raised in emergencies), or they could be formed into a fencible regiment. Many of the Highlanders were members of Clan Macdonell. Father Roderick Macdonell, a missionary to the Mohawks at nearby St. Regis (now Akwasasne), often visited the settlers. In addition to his plans for the Highlanders, Brock hoped to persuade the lieutenant-governor and commander of forces in both provinces, Lieutenant General Peter Hunter, to have the 41st Regiment, then in Montreal, move to the upper province.

Ahead for the 49th lay still more rapids. The most formidable was the Long Sault where the bateaux had to be unloaded and dragged up by the crews and soldiers. Other soldiers portaged all the baggage and supplies of provisions along a path on shore. Ahead lay

Rapide Plat and finally Galop, entailing less heavy work that was nonetheless still time-consuming.

The bateaux passed Prescott, named after the governor-in-chief, General Robert Prescott (who had been on leave in England since 1799 and had no intention of ever returning). Across the river, beside Ogdensburg, New York, they could see Fort Oswegatchie, which since 1796 had been in American hands. Under construction at Prescott was a stockade and the beginnings of a blockhouse, for protection in the event of war. Beyond the future Brockville lay the Thousand Islands, even then a hiding place for smugglers and ne'er do wells. At Kingston they could leave some of the bateaux, which would then be available to carry people and goods downriver.

They could continue along Lake Ontario in the small ships of the Provincial Marine. At Point Frederick lay a naval dockyard. Brock decided that, if he could obtain permission, he would have many armed ships built there to give him control of Lake Ontario. He would also look to Amherstburg for a dockyard to build ships for control of Lake Erie.

Before leaving Kingston, Brock had himself rowed to Carleton Island, close to the New York shore at the foot of Lake Ontario. It had the best harbour on the entire lake, overlooked by the now dilapidated Fort Haldimand, which had had a large garrison during the late revolution. Now it had a caretaker staff of a few men and two women. The main disadvantage to placing a new garrison there was Carleton Island's closeness to the United States. Having British troops so near, the Americans might be tempted to attack. The harbour at York was less vulnerable, which was why John Graves Simcoe had started to build the main naval base there.

For Brock, 1803 York was a depressing place, a collection of small houses, mostly of wood, and every time it rained the town became surrounded by oceans of mud, unusually heavy, sticky clay. Yet this little settlement was the capital, the place the elected legislative assembly met, and where the appointed legislative council held sway. The governor's executive council was chosen from among the most influential property owners. Constituencies were the counties. The government buildings were arranged at the intersection of Front and Parliament streets.

Fort York, to the west of the town, was a blockhouse, a collection of wooden huts where some of the garrison would sleep, and a powder magazine with thick brick walls, the whole enclosed by mounds of earth topped by a rickety stockade. In the complex was a single-storey officers' quarters. A similar structure was Government House.

Before he settled in, Brock had to deal with the problem of desertion. York was too convenient to the

M.B. Fryer.

View of Fort York, blockhouse on the left, one-storey officers' quarters, centre rear. This fort dates from 1816; it was rebuilt after the Americans attacked in April 1813.

lake, even though the harbour was enclosed by a peninsula, a sandbar with only a small opening at the western end. Fort York stood close to the opening, but with so many trees, hiding places were everywhere. He ordered guards for the three government boats that served the settlement, but keeping track of the boats in private ownership was nearly impossible.

The situation was even more serious at Fort George. This wooden fort had been built when Fort Niagara, across the narrow Niagara River, was given to the Americans in 1796. Before that time, the capital

Fort York Guard. Re-enacting has become popular at historic sites. Here the Fort York Guard, in red coats and grey trousers, are on the right. Units represented at marchpasts may be from other periods. The drummer on the left represents a Loyalist regiment 1777-1784. Between are some kilted Highlanders of the 78th Regiment, Seven Years' War 1756-1763.

John Graves Simcoe first chose had been Newark (Niagara-on-the-Lake). Once the capital was within range of the American guns at Fort Niagara, Simcoe had moved his government across the lake to the Toronto carrying place, renamed York. Desertion was even simpler from Fort George. Brock kept one wing — five companies — of the 49th at York, and sent the other five companies to the Niagara frontier, under the command of Lieutenant Colonel Roger Sheaffe. Perhaps, Brock reckoned, Sheaffe's stern discipline might make men hesitate to run away.

Gateway to Fort Niagara, Youngstown, New York. The fort Brock hoped to capture was built by the French, enlarged by the British, and handed to the United States in 1796. It is another popular site for re-enactors.

Desertion from Canadian frontier posts had always been a temptation for British regular troops. Across the water lay the promised land where they might be welcomed as new citizens and find more congenial work. Some even joined the tiny army of the United States. One evening Brock discovered that seven men of the 49th had stolen a boat and made off across the lake. Brock summoned James FitzGibbon, now his sergeant major, and twelve men to row, and set out in a bateau in pursuit. At Fort George he sent a party of officers to search along the United States shore, while he turned back to follow the Canadian shore. The other party apprehended the men on American soil and, with help from some Indians, brought them back to Canada. Here was a violation of the United States' sovereignty, but it was customary for each side to co-operate with the other.

The Americans were no happier when some of their own soldiers ran off to Canadian territory. Brock decided on a recommendation that would ease the situation. A regiment of older veterans would reduce desertions at frontier posts. The older men would not be suitable for hard duty, but they would be content with food, clothing, and shelter, and usually a pension, while watching neighbours who might turn unfriendly. Brock would use his powers of persuasion when next he went on leave.

Soon after the desertions from Fort York, Brock had to deal with a much graver situation at Fort George

84

— a planned mutiny. Officers sent a message secretly to Brock, naming a sergeant and a corporal reported to be ringleaders. The cause of the trouble was the harshness of Roger Sheaffe. Brock summoned a schooner and set out immediately for Fort George. Opening the gate for him were the suspected sergeant and corporal. He arrested both as conspirators.

He then censured Sheaffe for being "indiscreet and injudicious" in punishing men for minor lapses. He had reduced too many NCOs to the ranks. Sheaffe, Brock wrote, had "little knowledge of Mankind" and had acquired many enemies. Brock could not offer any reasons for Sheaffe's brutality, but the junior lieutenant colonel had friends among the Loyalist families who thought the hostility arose over Sheaffe's American origin. This raised doubts about his loyalty. Meanwhile, General Hunter ordered a court martial for the would-be mutineers and the deserters to be held in Quebec.

Lieutenant Colonel Sheaffe received an order to conduct the prosecution. He left for Quebec at the beginning of October. A few weeks earlier, in September, the chained prisoners had been led aboard a bateau for their journey. In command was Sergeant Major James FitzGibbon, who after the melancholy journey returned to York. Of those sent to Quebec, seven men were convicted: four for mutiny, and three for desertion. All were to be executed in Montreal, where the scene would have a more salutary effect on the troops stationed there. The date was set for March 2, 1804.

At Montreal the prisoners were lodged in the jail on Notre Dame Street, a short march from the Champs de Mars. The events that followed were recounted in the book on the records of the family compiled by Brock's nephew, Ferdinand Brock Tupper. He referred to a letter found in the possession of a captain in the 49th. Its author was not identified.

Major Alexander Campbell of the 41st and a party from that regiment, with one field gun, were the advance guard. Next came the firing party of fifty-six soldiers — eight per condemned man — carrying their muskets, powder, and shot. Behind were seven coffins drawn on wagons. Next came the men of the cloth, an escort of three Roman Catholic priests (a hint that some of the condemned were Irish) and "Mr. Mountain." The last was the Reverend Jehosophat, a brother of the Anglican Bishop of the Canadas, Jacob Mountain. To the sound of the drummers and fifers, Lieutenant Colonel Henry Procter, the commander of the 41st Foot, rode at the head of the main body of the regiment, with the colour party bearing the King's and regimental colours. Bringing up the rear were two companies of the 6th Regiment, along with seventy New Brunswick volunteers who marched without arms.

The prisoners were secured to poles, clad only in white shirt and trousers; the honour of a regimental identity was denied them. Everything went according to plan until the large firing party did not obey orders. Each group of eight faced its selected prisoner and began to walk towards him. They were ordered to hold their fire until they were within eight yards, to ensure that death would be instantaneous. No doubt all were nervous and under great strain, and shuddering with the thought that there but for the grace of God went they. Some fired at ten yards, some from as far away as fifty, and some did not fire at all. The seven were all alive, unhurt or slumped down from their poles writhing in agony. All the men who still had bullets in their muskets were ordered to move in close and finish off each of the condemned. The scene was an "awful and affecting sight" that made "a proper impression on the soldiers."

Roger Sheaffe no doubt believed that the seven, and probably many more, deserved execution. What apparently upset him most was the ease with which Brock assumed command when he reached Fort George, and how readily he soothed everyone else's feelings. More crushing was the cheer that rose from the throats of the 49th when they first spotted their respected leader. As one of the condemned men had admitted at the court martial, if Brock had been on the spot, there would never have been any attempt at rebellion.

Brock hated the whole experience. He knew the near mutiny should never have happened, but he did not sympathize with either deserter or mutineer. No matter what the provocation, such behaviour could not go unpunished. At stake was the regiment's fine long-term reputation, which he had worked hard to restore.

Before departing for York, Brock took time to study the surrounding land more closely. Fort Niagara stood on a promontory jutting into Lake Ontario. It could be seen from miles down the lake, while watchers from the ramparts would spot ships approaching. Fort George, no doubt for its safety, had been built further up the Niagara River, almost out of sight of Fort Niagara's guns, but not close enough to the lake for the garrison to keep a lookout. As commander of forces, General Hunter had ordered the construction of a stone light-house in full view of Fort Niagara. Brock would have preferred something stronger, with guns, but the light-house would be better than nothing. Watchers from that site would be able to alert Fort George of unusual activity on the American side of the Niagara River.

For guardians from the other direction posts, were located at Chippawa and Fort Erie. Manning both placed further strain on the meagre numbers of troops in Upper Canada. Chippawa lay above the "mountain," at the south end of the portage. The escarpment rose above the village of Queenston, down which dropped the great falls of the Niagara River. Fort Erie, where the Niagara River leaves Lake Erie, had been battered by severe winter storms since 1779. It needed to be rebuilt with solid masonry and further away from the lake itself. Brock was already worrying about the smallness of his garrisons, both as fighting forces and as workmen known as artificers.

CHAPTER SEVEN

Useful Years, 1804–07

As the dust gradually settled after the executions, the men of the 49th Regiment seemed more accepting. Brock was on the spot and Sheaffe appeared to be controlling his overbearing habits. The whole situation was cause for regret. Sheaffe was a more experienced field officer than Brock, and he also took care that no equipment or supplies were wasted. Having served at Fort Niagara before it changed hands, he well understood the difficulty of supplying posts so far inland. The small population of farmers did not produce enough food to feed the troops. Bateaux moving along the St. Lawrence were vulnerable to attack, while the Americans could easily slip across the Niagara and Detroit rivers.

Although no official census had yet been taken for either of the provinces, the population of Lower Canada was about three hundred thousand. That of Upper

Canada had been estimated at between sixty and eighty thousand, strung out over 1,660 kilometres (1,000 miles) in a thin line from the Cedars Rapids to Michilimackinac, most of the way through dense forests. All told, the population of British North America was not much more than half a million. The population of the United States had now reached nearly eight million. Any contest between far distant Britain and the United States would be very unequal. Of all the British provinces, Upper Canada was the most empty and the easiest to overrun.

For canoes and bateaux and the little ships of the Provincial Marine to reach the most western post required weeks of travel from the eastern border of Upper Canada. As most of the people were originally from the United States, Brock felt little confidence in their desire or ability to help in their own defence. He did not trust the Loyalists entirely, because many of them had maintained contact with their relatives who had stayed in the United States. As for the later arriving Americans, they had been lured by the prospect of cheap land. Many might welcome annexation to their homeland. (They have been called "Simcoe's Loyalists" because of his open door immigration policy.)

One cause for satisfaction was the arrival of Father Alexander Macdonell with some of his flock as new settlers for Glengarry County. The Glengarry Fencible Corps had helped put down the rebellion at

Wexford, Ireland, in 1798. After that action the corps was disbanded when the Treaty of Amiens brought a temporary peace between Britain and France. Father Macdonell again had to find a way to take care of the men and their families. He consulted with Prime Minister Henry Addington to assist him in helping his people emigrate.

Arrangements took time, but Macdonell and his people sailed for the Canadas in the summer of 1804. The government had promised two hundred acres for every man who went with him. Brock was overjoyed at the coming of such capable reinforcements. They could be useful in both Canadas, as they spoke only Gaelic. They could not be corrupted by American republican talk or by French-Canadian dissent.

At the same time, Brock desperately wanted to go home on leave. Letters took too long; replies might not come for four or more months. He could achieve more in a day in London than through a dozen letters. He was still uneasy about Sheaffe, but he had to trust him. His men would survive while he strove to persuade the government of the need to reinforce the defences of the Canadian frontier. About the time he received permission to go on leave, he was promoted to full colonel in the army. The commission was dated October 30, 1805, but on the Army List he remained, as well, the senior lieutenant colonel of the 49th Regiment.

While staying with his brother William in London, he drew up a detailed recommendation for coping with desertion and presented it to the War Office. He asked that a battalion of reliable old soldiers be formed for duty at border posts. His dream of some months past finally came true when the War Office agreed to establish the 10th Royal Veteran Battalion. Brock had started a system that would continue in the Canadian provinces through the rebellion era of the 1830s and '40s. (The system ended only when Canada took charge of defence in 1870 and the British army sailed for home.)

While Brock remained on leave, reports reaching him were alarming. They told of American restlessness over maritime rights. By British Orders-in-Council, the Royal Navy was blockading French ports, which interfered with American trade. Americans were also outraged because the Royal Navy was stopping American ships and searching them for deserters, or for men of British birth who could be "pressed into service" — forced to join the navy whether they wanted to or not. With life aboard His Majesty's ships so harsh, few men would volunteer to serve. For a country where so many of its people had been born in other countries, disregard of United States citizenship was an aberration.

At the same time unrest was growing among the French Canadians in Lower Canada. American settlers were still arriving in the upper province who, naturally, would side with their own countrymen should war be declared. Brock feared that many of the Loyalist founders of Upper Canada might not be relied upon for militia duty. To make matters worse, General Peter Hunter died soon after Brock reached England. Brock felt impelled to cut short his leave, and he sailed on June 28, 1806.

Arriving in Quebec in late August, Brock was at once placed in temporary command of all the troops in the Canadas to succeed Hunter. Upper Canada's new lieutenant-governor, Francis Gore, had reached York. The lieutenant-governor of Lower Canada was Robert Shore Milnes, who had arrived in 1799. While he was on the spot, he appeared to tolerate the language and religion of the majority to avoid controversy. Deep down he felt that assimilation of the French Canadians was ultimately the only way to ensure the stability of the colony. When Brock arrived, Milnes was on leave and had resigned. The Hon. Thomas Dunn, an elderly civilian, was the temporary administrator of Lower Canada. Brock wasted no time in preparing a defence for the two provinces. As Quebec was the gateway, making it secure was a first priority in protecting lines of communication to Britain. Cut off, both provinces could easily fall into American hands.

At this point, Brock's voice became stronger. His nephew, Ferdinand Brock Tupper, discovered a trunk and a box full of his uncle's clothing, but more important, Brock's correspondence dating from 1806, which Ferdinand edited and published.

On October 28, 1806, Brock wrote to the Hon. William Windham, secretary of state for war and the colonies, outlining his plans and activities. He required a proper military hospital at Quebec. There were few houses of any sort for rent. He sent a drawing of a plan for a suitable hospital building. With the extremes of temperatures in Quebec, wooden huts would not do. They were stifling in summer heat and in winter the bitter winds whistled through the cracks no matter how well they were chinked. Captain Ralph Henry Bruyere, the commanding Royal Engineer, proposed using a site being held for a barracks by Major General Gother Mann, an officer in the Royal Engineers, who was inspector of fortifications.

To Windham, Brock sent a list of the boats — bateaux — to be maintained: six at Quebec, two at Three Rivers, one at Fort William Henry at the entrance to the Richelieu River, seven at Montreal, two at St. John's (St. Jean), four at Kingston, twelve at Fort George, three at York, and four at Amherstburg — forty-one in all.

Work parties reconstructed walls facing the Plains of Abraham. Others built an elevated battery with eight heavy guns — Brock's battery — at the temporary citadel that had been erected during the American Revolution. From the citadel it commanded the south side of the St.

Lawrence. Then he turned to the militia. Of the estimated population of Lower Canada at three hundred thousand, on paper he could collect the names of every man between ages sixteen and sixty, but names on lists did not translate into armed, trained men. Training took time. Arms were almost non-existent, apart from those reserved for regular soldiers. Unwillingness to serve cut down numbers still more.

All Brock's enterprises cost money. He was soon in disfavour with the civilian government of Lower Canada and the administrator, whom he addressed as "Mr. President Dunn" in a letter dated January 5, 1807. Brock was protesting against encroachments on military land — tracts reserved for future requirements that should not be built on by civilians and lost to the army. For his part, Dunn disapproved of Brock's using a piece of land near the Jesuit College for drill.

Brock was also responsible for the cost of the Indian Department. The goodwill of the First Nations people was necessary. They would be allies in the event of open war with the Americans. Brock wanted a civilian labour force to work on the fortifications. He needed to call out the militia for training — a volunteer force, authorized and armed, called the embodied militia.

A very worried Dunn gave him little co-operation. As Dunn grew more cautious, Brock's frustrations mounted.

Of slight compensation was the social life. High-ranking officers, especially those who spoke acceptable French, mingled with the elite of Quebec society, the land-holding *seigneurs*. They could be equally at ease with the wealthy English minority who prospered through trade and commerce.

On January 27, from Quebec, Brock wrote to Lieutenant-Governor Gore at York concerning the "management of the Indians." Gore was to follow His Majesty's instructions of December 15, 1794, which had placed the sole control of the First Nations people in the lieutenant-governor's hands. Where Gore advanced money, his signature was all that was required. Government policy was to keep the warriors content. Soon they might be needed.

On February 12 Brock was again writing to Secretary Windham, stating his case for a corps of fencibles. For the chaplain he recommended his respected colleague Father Alexander Macdonell, now settled with some of his flock among other Macdonells. Brock proposed having Lieutenant Colonel John "M'Donell" raise a corps among the Scots of Glengarry County, Upper Canada, to increase the military force to be stationed in Lower Canada and check the "seditious disposition" around Montreal. The Reverend Alexander "M'Donell" would be suitable as so many of the Highlanders were Roman Catholics.

In making his request Brock was fulfilling another dream: a way to increase the military strength of the Canadas. Just who he meant by John M'Donell is not clear, because so many of that clan had been named John. He may have meant Captain "Red George" Macdonell, who had served in the 8th Regiment, and who would command the Glengarry Light Infantry Fencibles in 1812.

By July, he warned Dunn that he expected a rupture between Britain and the United States owing to the new Embargo Act, which the American congress had passed in retaliation for the British Orders-in-Council. The Act forbade American ships to leave for foreign ports. Foreign ships could unload in American ports, but were not permitted to carry goods out of American ports. The measure was ineffective and very unpopular with traders. At Sackets Harbor, New York, angry Americans tried to prevent government interference with the trade across Lake Ontario and along the St. Lawrence River. Their armed guards accompanied timber rafts down Lake Champlain and the Richelieu to ensure that they reached Quebec. Owners of forest could become wealthy, but only if they had access to Quebec, because logs could not float upstream.

Brock had found one important job that he could do without interference. He was also the deputy quartermaster general, which gave him a free hand to reform

the Provincial Marine. He would create his own fighting navy. Until now, the Provincial Marine had been
used to transport people and supplies through the
Great Lakes. He would improve the dockyards at Point
Frederick, Kingston, and Amherstburg by appointing a
quartermaster general at each port to oversee the construction of the new fleets. The flagship of the fleet on
Lake Ontario would be the *Royal George,* a miniature
full-rigged ship. Others soon under construction were
the *Earl of Moira,* the *Duke of Gloucester,* the *Wolfe,* the
Prince Regent, and the *Princess Charlotte.*

The way between the two dockyards was blocked by
Niagara Falls, where supplies and men had to travel over
the high, very long portage. Among the first new ships
launched at Amherstburg were the *Queen Charlotte* and
the *Hunter,* the latter named in honour of the late commander of troops.

For armament Brock scrounged wherever he could —
at Chimney Island, New York (the former French Fort
Lévis), and at Carleton Island and Kingston itself. For the
Lake Erie fleet he tracked down some pieces at Fort Erie.
Ships from Amherstburg could sail all the way to
Michilimackinac, a wider territory but apart from Detroit,
with very few inhabitants, except for the Native nations.

Brock's many projects involved considerable travelling. He wanted to inspect all the works he had authorized, which meant covering Quebec City and Montreal,

both sides of the St. Lawrence, and down the Richelieu as far as Fort Chambly and Isle aux Noix at the bottom of Lake Champlain. He sent orders to the posts in Upper Canada and demanded reports to keep him informed on how the work was progressing. He longed to travel as far as Amherstburg and, if possible, the fort on St. Joseph's Island. For the time being, his duties kept him from going further west than Lachine.

Brock wrote to Dunn on July 7 that he had only three hundred militia armed and trained. Many thousands more should be formed into regiments. He also needed from "60 to 1,000 workers per day for six weeks to two months," and many carts, to complete the defences around Quebec.

By the autumn, everyone knew that a new governor-in-chief had been appointed. He arrived at Quebec on October 24 aboard the ship of the line *Horatio*. Lieutenant General Sir James Henry Craig, K.B., was an officer of great experience in North America. He had served during the American Revolution and afterwards. Two versions remain about his arrival. One was that he disembarked with great pomp and ceremony to a fifteen-gun salute before a large crowd. The newspaper *Canadien*, with classical allusion, suggested the coming of a second Hannibal, who would purge a clique being dubbed the Canadian Carthage. The British residents hoped for a resolute policy favouring themselves. The

French Canadians expected the righting of what they saw as wrongs.

The second version of Craig's arrival came from Brock's nephew. Craig had asked for his landing to be private. He hoped to be taken to the citadel quickly, out of fear of a French-Canadian rising. Craig came wanting to establish good relations with the First Nations. If the British and Canadians did not make use of them as allies, the Americans certainly would. As time went by, Craig stirred up many bad feelings among the French Canadians over his outspoken policy of assimilation. His time in the Canadas has been called "Craig's Reign of Terror," a view Brock did not share.

To Brock, Craig was, like himself, a professional soldier. Their relationship was sometimes abrupt, but usually businesslike. Craig was unwell when he arrived. Once he was feeling stronger, he promoted Brock to the local rank of brigadier general. This meant that he was still a colonel in the army, and still the commander of the 49th Regiment.

Now that Craig was commander of all the troops, he sent Brock to assume military command in Montreal. The residence of the governor stood on Notre Dame Street near Bonsecours. The house was comfortable and the posting would be pleasant socially. But Brock was disappointed at being sent to Montreal when he was anxious to be in Upper Canada. The 49th was still stationed at York and Fort George, and he hated being separated from his men. He was also missing the company of his brother Savery, who had left the 49th and would soon be in Portugal with Wellington's army.

CHAPTER EIGHT

Limbo: Montreal and Quebec, 1808–1810

Brock did not stay long in Montreal. A letter from Montreal to his brothers was dated July 20, 1808. His next letter was sent from Quebec on September 5. He had been superceded at Montreal by Major General Gordon Drummond, who had served in the Netherlands, the West Indies, and Egypt.

Brock did not seem to have a specific job, but his letters reveal activities, opinions, friendships, family relationships, frustrations, and the state of his health. When he wrote the first of the following letters, Roger Sheaffe was brevet colonel in the army and in command of the 49th Regiment at York and Fort George.

Brock to his brothers, Montreal, July 20, 1808

I have written to all of you since the navigation opened [the ice melted], and the only letters I have received from any of the family for several months came from Irving who to do him justice, is infinitely the most attentive and regular correspondent among you.

My appointment to be brigadier I first announced by the March mail. Those who feel an interest in my prosperity will rejoice in my good fortune, as this distinguished mark of favor affords undeniable proof that my conduct, during the period of my command, was approved — a great gratification, considering the many difficulties I had to encounter.

I once thought I should be ordered to the upper province, but General Ferguson being among the newly appointed major-generals, will not now probably visit this country. In that case I stand a very good chance of succeeding him both in rank and in command of Quebec, where it was intended he should be stationed.[2]

What will be the result of our present unsettled relations with the neighbouring republic, it is very difficult to say. The government is composed of such unprincipled men, that to calculate on it by the ordinary rules of action would be perfectly absurd.

---

2. Ferguson went to Portugal and served as one of Wellington's brigade commanders.

We have completely outwitted Jefferson in all his schemes to provoke us to war.[3] He had no other view in using his restrictive proclamation; but failing in that, he tried what the embargo would produce, and there he has been foiled again.

Certainly, our administration is deserving of every praise for their policy on these occasions. Jefferson and his party, however strong the inclination, dare not declare war, and therefore they endeavour to attain their object by every provocation.

A few weeks since, the [United States] garrison of Niagara fired upon seven merchant boats passing the fort, and actually captured them. Considering the circumstances attending this hostile act, it is but too evident it was intended to provoke retaliation: these boats fired upon and taken within musket shot of our own fort [Fort George]; their balls falling on our shore, was expected to have raised the indignation of the most phlegmatic; fortunately, the commandant was not in the way, as otherwise it is difficult to say what would have happened.

A representation of this affair has been made at Washington, and, for an act certainly opposed to existing treaties, we have been referred for justice to the ordinary course of the law. If our subjects cannot com-

---

3. Thomas Jefferson was president of the United States from 1801 to 1809. He was responsible for The Embargo Act of 1807.

mand impunity [immunity] from capture under the guns of our own forts, it were better to demolish them at once rather than witness and suffer such indignity. By the treaties which have expired, the navigation of the waters that divide the two countries is regulated and stipulated to be still in force, although every other part should cease to be obligatory.

I get on pretty well, but this place [Montreal] loses at this season the undoubted advantage it possesses over Quebec in winter. Great additions are making to fortifications at Quebec, and, when completed the Americans will, if I mistake not, think it prudent not to trouble the place, for they can have no chance of making any impression upon it during the short period which the severity of the climate only permits an enemy to lay before it.

I erected, as I believe I told you before, a famous battery, which the public voice named after me; but Sir James [Craig], thinking very probably that any thing so very pre-eminent should be distinguished by the most exalted appellation, has called it the King's Battery, the greatest compliment I conceive, that he could pay.

Not a desertion has been attempted by any of the 49th for the last ten months, with the exception of Hogan, Savery's former servant. He served [Major John] Glegg in the same capacity, who took him with him to the

Falls of Niagara, where a fair damsel persuaded him to this act of madness, for the fool cannot possibly gain his bread by labour, as he has half killed himself with excessive drinking; and we know he cannot live upon love alone.

The weather has been exceedingly hot the last week, the thermometer fluctuating from 94 to 100 [degrees Fahrenheit] in the shade. The embargo has proved a famous harvest to some merchants here. It is certainly the most ridiculous measure imaginable, and was evidently adopted with the view of pleasing France; but no half measure can satisfy Napoleon, and this colony has been raised by it to a degree of importance that ensures its future prosperity.

Brock to his brothers, Quebec, September 5, 1808

I have been here but a few days, having been superceded at Montreal by Major General [Gordon] Drummond. I do not approve much of the change as being separated from the 49th is a great annoyance to me. But soldiers must accustom themselves to frequent movements; and as they have no choice, it often happens that they are placed in situations little agreeing with their inclinations. My nominal appointment has been confirmed at home, so that I am really a brigadier. Were the 49th ordered hence, the rank would not be a sufficient inducement to keep me in this country. In such a case, I would throw it up willingly.[4]

Curious scenes appear to have occurred in the Baltic. I fear very much for Sir James [Saumarez], may be induced to return to his retirement in Guernsey.[5] Indeed, the navy has little left to do while the army has now a glorious opportunity of distinguishing itself as much as the sister service. Valour the British troops allways possessed, but unless they evince discipline, their fame will be blasted for a century to come.

Brock to his brothers, Quebec, November 19, 1808

Yesterday Irving's letter of the 19th September reached me. How very thankful I feel for his attention. But I have not received that which he mentions. Savery had written on the same date, giving an account of his proceedings in Spain and Portugal. This is a truly mortifying disappointment, as it is impossible to discover by the public prints [newspapers] the mystery by which the conduct of our officers has been influenced.

---

4. He implies that he would resume the rank of colonel in order to remain with the regiment.

5. Captain Sir James Saumarez, later an admiral in the Royal Navy, was a brother of Susan Saumarez, the wife of Isaac's uncle, Henry Brock.

The precaution Irving took to transcribe a part of the letter has proved very lucky. Notwithstanding, I look for the original with unusual impatience, as Savery's opinion must be formed upon what he saw in the best disciplined army that ever, I imagine, left England. His observations are never thrown away.

I am still confined to my room, more indeed on account of the badness of the weather than any want of progress in my recovery. We have had very hard gales from the East. The *Iphigenia* frigate, with her convoy, could not have cleared the land, and the greatest apprehension is entertained for her safety.

Her commander, Captain [Henry] Lambert is a friend of George Brock [a cousin]. I find him an exceedingly good fellow; and I have reason to think that he left us well satisfied with the attention he received from me.

Sir James Craig has certain intimation of the appointment of Colonel [Francis] de Rottenburg, of the 60th [Regiment] to be a brigadier in this country, and he is daily looked for. This most probably will make a change in my situation, as one [of us] must go to the Upper Province; and as he is senior, he will doubtless have the choice.

My object is to get home as soon as I can obtain permission; but unless our affairs with Americans be amicably adjusted, of which I see no probability, I scarcely can expect to be permitted to leave.

I rejoice Savery has begun to exert himself to get me appointed to a more active situation. I must see service, or I may as well, and indeed much better, quit the army at once, for no one advantage can I reasonably look to hereafter if I remain buried in this inactive remote corner, without the least mention being made of me. Should Sir James Saumarez return from the Baltic crowned with success, he could, I should think, say a good word for me to some purpose.[6]

Brock to his brother William, Quebec, December 31, 1809

You will long since have been convinced that the American government is determined to involve the two countries in a war; they have already given us legitimate cause, but, if wise, we will studiously avoid doing that for which they shew so great an anxiety.

---

6.   Some appointments of officers at the Horse Guards were political, not necessarily deserving. Sources say that Brock had risen exceptionally rapidly although he did not have powerful friends at the Horse Guards. On this occasion, desperate to leave the "Canadian backwater," Brock was looking for a benefactor or protector. (John Graves Simcoe's benefactor had been Henry Addington, while he was prime minister. Addington also helped Father Macdonell when he wanted to immigrate to Glengarry County, Upper Canada.)

Their finances, you will perceive, are very low, and they dare not propose direct taxes. They must have recourse to loans at a time when they have only six frigates in commission, and about five thousand men embodied. To what a state of poverty and wretchedness would the accumulated expenses of war reduce them!

But they look to the success of their privateers for a supply, and contemplate the sweeping away of all foreign debts as the means of reducing the calls upon their treasury. Whatever steps England may adopt, I think she cannot in prudence, avoid sending a strong military force to these provinces, as they are now become of infinite importance to her.

You can scarcely conceive the quantities of timber and spars [masts for the Royal Navy ships] of all kinds which are lying on the beach, ready for shipment to England in the spring; four hundred vessels would not be sufficient with these essential articles, but from the Canadas!

Bonaparte, it is known, has expressed a strong desire to be in possession of the colonies formerly belonging to France, and now that they are become so valuable to England, his anxiety to wrest them from us will naturally increase. A small French force, 4 or 5,000 men with plenty of muskets, would most assuredly conquer this province. The [French speaking] Canadians would join them almost to a man — at least the exceptions would be so low as to be of little avail.

It may appear surprising that men, petted as they have been and indulged in every thing they could desire, should wish for a change. But so it is — and I am apt to think that were Englishmen placed in the same situation, they would shew even more impatience to escape from French rule.

How essentially different are the feelings of the [French-speaking] people from when I first knew them. The idea prevails generally among them that Napoleon must succeed, and ultimately get possession of these provinces. The bold and violent are becoming every day more audacious; and the timid, with that impression, think it better and more prudent to withdraw altogether from the society of the English, rather than run the chance of being accused hereafter of partiality to them.

The consequence is that little or no intercourse exists between the two races. More troops will be required in this country, were it only to keep down this growing turbulent spirit.[7] The governor will, it is foreseen, have a dif-

---

7. In his letters Brock did not admit that Sir James Craig's policies were largely responsible for French-Canadian discontent. Intolerant both of the Roman Catholic religion and the French culture, Craig was determined to eliminate all vestiges of the legacy of France. He strove to force assimilation into the Protestant religion and the English language. Modern Quebec historians claim that Craig's tactics laid the foundation of French-Canadian nationalism. Brock was an observer of the result, although he did not appear to recognize that Craig, who was his friend, was to blame.

ficult card to play next month with the assembly, which is really getting too daring and arrogant. Every victory which Napoleon has gained for the last nine years, has made the disposition here to resist more manifest.

Brock to Mrs. William Brock, Quebec, June 8, 1810

It was my decided intention to ask for leave to go to England this fall, but I have now relinquished the thought. Several untoward circumstances combine to oppose my wishes. The spirit of insubordination lately manifested by the French Canadian population of this colony naturally called for precautionary measures; and our worthy chief [Craig] is induced, in consequence to retain in this country those on whom he can best confide. I am highly flattered in being reckoned among the number, whatever events have likewise happened in the upper country, which have occasioned my receiving intimation to proceed thither, whether as a permanent station, or merely as a temporary visit, Sir James Craig has not determined.

Should, however, a senior brigadier to myself come out in the course of the summer, I shall certainly be fixed in the upper Province, and there is every probability of such an addition very soon. Since all my efforts to get more actively employed have failed; since fate decrees that the best portion of my life is to be wasted in inaction in the Canadas, I am rather pleased with the prospect of removing upwards.[8]

There is a lady living at Barnet [a suburb of London] for whom I feel much interested. If you should by chance drive that way, and do not object to form a new acquaintance, I wish you to call upon her. She is the wife of Captain [Thomas] Manners, of the 49th, and the daughter of a celebrated Dr. Rush of Philadelphia. She has a most amiable disposition and genteel manners. Her sister, Mrs. Ross Cuthbert, a charming little creature, makes her husband — my most intimate friend, and with whom I pass a great part of my leisure hours — a most happy man.

I received the other day a long and exceedingly well written letter from Henrietta Tupper — she is really a charming girl. What! Marie [Potenger, daughter of Brock's sister Marie] do you begin to slacken in your attention to your poor devoted uncle?

Brock to his brother Irving, Quebec, July 9, 1810

I have a thousand thanks to offer you for the very great attention you have shewn in executing my commissions;

---

8.   Seniority applied to appointments from the list of brigadier generals by date, much as promotions in regiments were by seniority.

the different articles arrived in the very best order, with the exception of the cocked hat, which has not been received — a most distressing circumstance, as, from the enormity of my head, I find the utmost difficulty in getting a substitute in this country.

I proposed writing to you early to-morrow, but Sir James having this instant intimated his intention of sending me upwards [to Upper Canada] immediately, I avail myself of an hour's leisure to do that hastily which I would gladly have done quietly, and, consequently, more fully. If I am to remain in this country, I care little where I am placed: but going up, as I do now, without knowing whether I am to stay or return, is particularly awkward, and interferes materially in all my future arrangements; perhaps I shall be able to get the point settled before I commence my journey.

Everything here remains in a state of perfect quietness. It is but too evident that the Canadians generally are becoming daily more anxious to get rid of the English. This they cannot effect unless a French force come to their aid, and I do not think that Bonaparte would risk the loss of a fleet and army for the chance of getting possession of the country.

What infatuation! No people had ever more cause to rejoice at their fate; but they are not singular, as all mankind seems prone to change, however disadvantageous or productive of confusion.

Savery forwarded your pamphlet to me. You have taken a very proper view of the political dissenters which at this moment disgrace England. Those on whom I have allowed a perusal, and who are infinitely better judges than I can pretend to be, speak of the purity of the language in terms of high approbation.

You have happily suited the style to the matter. Several copies have, within a few days, been in circulation here. Savery speaks of a letter you received in consequence, from Lord Melville.[9] I hope you will not fail in sending me a copy, as I am all anxiety for your literary fame. As you differ in sentiment from the *Edinburgh Review*, I hope that you have made up your mind to an unmerciful lashing.

I do not see the smallest prospect of my getting away from here, as the disposition manifested by the Canadians will occasion a large military force to be kept in the country, and it will serve as a plea to retain all their posts. I wish that I could boast of a little more patience than I feel I now possess.

The fortifications of Quebec are improving pretty rapidly, but workmen cannot be procured in sufficient number to proceed as fast as government would wish. Labourers now get 7s. 6d. [seven shillings and sixpence] a day, and artificers [skilled construction work-

---

9. Lord Melville was the former Henry Dundas, secretary of state for the colonies, 1794–1801, later created the first Viscount Melville.

ers] 12s. to 15s. Upwards of three hundred vessels have already arrived, a prodigious number.[10]

Brock was indeed feeling gloomy, as though the past years had been a waste of his life. By 1810 his luck was beginning to change.

10. The vessels were the supply fleet from Britain on which the Canadas depended to supplement the food and materials that could be produced locally.

PART III

Upper Canada
1810–1812

CHAPTER NINE

Commander of Forces and Administrator

By July 1810, Brock felt he still faced an uncertain future. Governor Craig had ordered him to set out for the upper country without delay. While his aide-de-camp and his servant, Dobson, were preparing for the bateau journey up the St. Lawrence, Brock dashed off a letter to his sister-in-law, Mrs. William Brock.

Brock to Mrs. William Brock, Quebec, July 10, 1810

I cannot allow the frigate to depart without sending my affectionate love to you. A Guernsey vessel arrived a few days ago, which brought me a letter from Savery of 10th May, and nothing could be more gratifying than the contents. The May fleet, which sailed from Portsmouth on 24th, reached this in thirty days, but as it had not a scrape of a pen for me, its arrival did not interest me.

We have been uncommonly gay the last fortnight: two frigates at anchor, and the arrival of Governor Gore from the Upper Province, have given a zest to society. Races, country and water parties, have occupied our time in a continued round of festivity. Such stimulus is highly necessary to keep our spirits afloat. I contributed my share to the general mirth in a grand dinner given for Mrs. Gore, at which Sir J. Craig was present, and a ball to a vast assemblage of all descriptions.

I mentioned in a former letter my apprehension of being ordered to the Upper Province. I return this moment from waiting upon Sir James, who sent for me, to say he regretted he must part with me, as he found it absolutely necessary that I should proceed upwards without delay. I am placed in a very awkward predicament, as my stay in that country depends wholly upon contingencies. Should a brigadier arrive, I am to be stationary, but otherwise return to Quebec. Nothing could be more provoking and inconvenient than this arrangement. Unless I take up everything with me, I shall be miserably off, for nothing beyond eatables is to be had there ...

Governor Craig had no such concerns over whether Brock would stay in Upper Canada, and for reasons he had not shared with his subordinate. After interviewing Lieutenant-Governor Francis Gore, he realized that he was not experienced enough to instill a fighting spirit in a province that must be prepared to defend itself. War was inevitable. Gore had served in the army and retired as a major in 1802, after the Treaty of Amiens. He had not returned to the army when that peace was broken in 1803 by Napoleon's declaration of war against Britain. Gore did not know how to raise the militia and have the men trained, clothed, and equipped. Brock would go as commander of forces, while Gore would attempt to deal with civil matters.

Gore had not been getting along well with his legislators. The lieutenant-governor could accept or reject bills passed by the assembly and he could overrule his councils. The government was representative in that the members of the assembly were elected. The government — the legislature — was not responsible because it could be ignored. Most of the white residents were apathetic. Conquest could be accomplished by what former president Thomas Jefferson was calling "a mere matter of marching." The election of 1808 had been won by James Madison. Americans who were against attacking Canada would dub the conflict "Mr. Madison's War."

The members of the Iroquois nations who had settled in Canada after the American Revolution were cool to the idea of becoming involved in a fight with the

Americans. Parts of their own nations had remained in the United States, and they did not want to go to war against their own people. Those who were living along the Grand River were arguing amongst themselves over how to administer their land. Some wanted permission to sell land because that was their right as the owners. Others were using the Royal Proclamation of 1763 and the Quebec Act of 1774 to block sales. The Proclamation and the Act were intended by the British government to prevent disposing of land that might ultimately deprive the nations of land their own people needed. Brock was worried that the Iroquois might decide to stay neutral if either side declared war. Nations further west and north were a worry because they were actively talking of remaining neutral.

To Brock the situation did not look promising. Of his estimate of eighty thousand men, women, and children in Upper Canada, some thirteen thousand were Loyalists, and another fourteen thousand traced their families directly to the British Isles. That left some fifty-one thousand of American origin who had come mainly in the 1790s — more than half the residents of Upper Canada. Of the other colonies of British North America: in addition to the three hundred thousand in Lower Canada, another eighty thousand were in Nova Scotia, New Brunswick, Prince Edward Island, and Newfoundland. This made half a million in British North America to defend themselves against a nation whose population was approaching eight million.

Upper Canada, Brock remembered, with its long border and dense forests, was the most vulnerable part. He had every intention of strengthening a defence. His hopes lay in reports brought by informers of the lack of preparation evident on the other side of the border. He had the advantage of the armed ships of the Provincial Marine — mobility on water — and water travel was the best means of travel during the campaign season. The Americans needed to build decent roads to reach the Great Lakes. The enemy would have more difficulty supplying their bases than Brock would his.

Brock travelled with Major John Glegg, his aide-de-camp. At the border between the upper and lower provinces, they were joined by their escort of the 49th, who had come down from Kingston. The villages they passed looked better than in 1803, and the tracks beside the rapids were smoother. Brock stopped briefly at Cornwall, where a young Scotsman, the Reverend John Strachan, was operating a school. Strachan had come to Upper Canada in 1799 as a schoolmaster. He worked first at Kingston. After he took holy orders in 1803, he received the parish of Cornwall. Brock was impressed with the quality of instruction Strachan described. He had some twenty boys enrolled, but Brock met only five or six who lived at home. The others, who boarded in the village, had departed for the summer holidays.

Farmer pioneers were growing more wheat than they could market. Making spirituous liquor required a licence, but many were operating stills in the backwoods and smuggling their whiskey across the river for sale to thirsty Americans. The story of Brock's supposed stop to name Brockville may be in doubt, but he left evidence of time spent in Kingston.

He was welcomed by many prominent citizens, including Richard Cartwright, Loyalist and successful merchant and trader, and Thomas Fuller, the Anglican rector of St. George's Church. He agreed to be godfather to the Fullers' newborn son, who was duly baptized Thomas Brock Fuller. Brock felt honoured. He longed for the day when he would have children of his own. First he had to accumulate enough money to retire from the army and find the right Guernsey lady for his wife. (Years after, Thomas Brock Fuller became the first Anglican Bishop of the diocese of Niagara.)

Brock found the 49th distributed in three places. At Kingston was a detachment under Lieutenant Colonel John Vincent. Some were at York, while the others were with Sheaffe on the Niagara Frontier. Those under Sheaffe were not happy. Sergeant Major James FitzGibbon had been keeping records:

Corporal James Doran 28 March 1810. He was accused of defrauding some soldiers' wives of part of the bread issued for them. The sentence was 100 lashes, but it was not recorded as having been carried out.

After numerous entries for being "Drunk before morning parade although confined to barracks." The sentence was 200 lashes, 150 inflicted.

For "Quitting the barracks without leave after tatoo." The sentence was 300 lashes, 295 inflicted.

John Turner 4 April 1810. He was punished for having in his possession some pease [peas} for which he cannot honestly account, and for making an improper use of the barrack bedding. 400 lashes, 250 inflicted.

Edward Marraly 15 November 1810. For being deficient of a shirt, part of regimental necessaries. 200 lashes, 75 inflicted.

Private Patrick Lallagan 26 Jan. 1811. For being deficient in drill, part of his regimental necessaries. 100 lashes, no record of how many inflicted.

13 February 1811. Deficient of a razor, part of his regimental necessaries, and for producing a razor belonging to Private James Rooney, thereby attempting to deceive the inspecting officer. 200 lashes, 100 inflicted.

Also put under stoppages of one shilling per week until the razor was replaced.

The number of lashes laid on were often lower than the sentence, where a surgeon ruled that a man could take no more. In some cases that was the end of the punishment, but in others the rest of the sentence might be carried out once the man had recovered.

Brock was no longer in a position to temper Sheaffe's discipline. When he was promoted brigadier general he ceased to perform the duties of senior lieutenant colonel of the 49th.

That autumn of 1810 Brock began collecting returns on the militia. On paper he had eleven thousand men between sixteen and sixty, but he felt that not more than four thousand could be trusted. He could not hope to provide sufficient training for four thousand men, or about eight battalions, but he could expect to use some volunteers from each battalion as flank companies. This meant usually the light and grenadier companies. The rest of the battalion could rally around the more highly trained men. The flank companies would meet for six days each month for intensive drill, but without extra pay. To begin with, each flank company would have one captain, two subalterns, two sergeants, one drummer, and thirty-five rank and file.

The winter passed in drill, weather permitting, and work on the defences at Kingston, where a blockhouse was nearing completion at Point Henry, and improvements were being made to the stockades at Fort York, Fort George, Chippawa, Fort Erie, Fort Malden, and Fort St. Joseph on St. Joseph's Island. From the latter a watch could be kept on the Americans at Michilimackinac.

To his brother Irving he wrote of the loneliness of the posting, of the dearth of books of any sort other than the Bible. He asked Irving to send him a good selection — *Plutarch's Lives*, for instance. He still hoped to be ordered home so that he could serve under Lord Wellington in Portugal or Spain.

His complaints about the lack of regular troops continued. Yet he knew perfectly well that few could be spared for duty in the Canadas, not when the British army was fully occupied combatting Napoleon and his tough battalions. Spring brought some relief for the 49th Regiment. In July 1811 both Brock and Sheaffe were promoted to major general. Sheaffe went to England on leave. He was perturbed that he would have only a lieutenant colonel's pay, but the promotion to major general implied higher expenses. Brock had no such complaints. Sheaffe had a wife and children, but Brock could manage quite nicely on the pay of a colonel. John Vincent was now the commander, as senior lieutenant colonel of the 49th. Brock regarded Kingston, where Vincent would soon be stationed, as the most secure base in the upper province. He found the militia in the neighbourhood more enthusiastic, because of a strong United Empire Loyalist element. He was changing his opinion of their abilities as soldiers. At last he was discovering that Loyalists had been soldiers and soldiers' wives and children. Those living along the St. Lawrence were more alarmed by the nearness of their American neighbours than the people around York.

About the same time, in June 1811, Sir James Craig had become seriously ill and had asked to be relieved. Before he sailed he sent Brock a gift that delighted him: Craig's favourite horse, named Alfred.

During the summer Brock became better acquainted with the Gores. Annabella was sometimes called Lady Gore, although her husband was neither a knight nor a baronet. Titled or not, both Gores were well-connected gentlefolk who improved the tone of the social life of Muddy York. They were pleased to loan books that helped Brock pass the long evenings. Yet Gore himself was becoming more and more discouraged with the bickering within the assembly and councils. Mrs. Gore, however, continued spreading goodwill and enjoying herself. She charmed Brock, who wrote to his family in Guernsey of his fondness for her.

Word from Guernsey by August left Brock deeply upset and worried. In June, William and Irving's firm of bankers and their mercantile pursuits had both failed. Part of the cause was the blockades that made trade so risky. The whole family was affected. Ferdinand Brock Tupper recalled that his father had been ruined. He had lost between £12,000 and £13,000, and he had eleven children. Savery had also lost some, and there was coolness between William and Irving. The family was shattered. Brock's personal loss was £3,000, money William had advanced him to purchase his commissions. Although the money was in effect a gift, the sum had been left on the firm's books and Isaac was deemed responsible for the payment of this debt. He could do little to help; he needed his pay as a colonel to cover his own expenses. What worried him most was the prospect of quarrelling that would destroy the traditional harmony existing among his relatives. From the great distance, Isaac could offer mainly sympathy through letters.

Autumn brought important changes in leadership. Lieutenant-Governor and Mrs. Gore departed on an extended leave of absence, and Brock became the administrator of Upper Canada. The Gores made a stop at Kingston, where they met the Reverend John Strachan. The lieutenant-governor offered the promising clergyman the parish of York, for which he had received permission from Bishop Jacob Mountain. Happy to accept, Strachan prepared to move his school to York and to become the rector of St. James's Church. Brock approved, and he decided to appoint Strachan the chaplain of the garrison at York.

As administrator of Upper Canada, Brock's salary was £1,000 per year. He signed this amount over to his youngest brother, Irving, to pay down the debt or use to assist the family, whichever Irving chose. He would manage, as he had done while serving as colonel and as commander of forces. His wage as colonel amounted to 22s. and 6d. per day, with no increase when he took over the forces.

Sir James Craig's replacement was Lieutenant General Sir George Prevost, who was born in New Jersey in 1767. He was the eldest son of Augustin Prevost, who had commanded a battalion of the 60th Regiment during the Seven Years' War and had remained in North America for some years afterward.

The Prevost family were French-speaking Swiss Protestants, thus Sir George could have a foot in each camp. As Protestants they were acceptable to the English in the colony, while as francophones they pleased the Canadians. Sir George Prevost was to be the antidote to Sir James Craig, to convince the Canadians that they would not be forced to abandon their religion and mother tongue. In accordance with British policy as war with the United States loomed larger, Prevost was also a professional soldier. So was Sir James Craig, but Prevost was of a very different character. He would soothe where Craig had ruffled.

Prevost, who had been serving as lieutenant-governor of Nova Scotia, arrived as president, and as administrator of Lower Canada to replace Thomas Dunn. On October 21, 1811, he was commissioned governor-in-chief of British North America. He was committed to a policy of appeasement. With so little help available, he dared not wage war. Although he had been a commissioned officer since his ensigncy in 1779, Prevost had had very little experience as a commander of an army in the field. His strength lay in his ability to conserve, to shepherd his resources carefully. He was, above all, cautious. Tensions between Brock and Prevost were inevitable.

LAKE SUPERIOR
(Whitefish Bay)

30 kilometres
19 miles

Sault Ste. Marie Rapids
Lock for canoes destroyed by U.S.
troops later in War of 1812)

MICHIGAN TERRITORY

◻**Michilimackinac Island**

Straits of Mackinac
LAKE
MICHIGAN   MICHIGAN   Bois Blanc Island
TERR.   *LAKE HURON*
LOCATION OF MICHILIMACKINAC ISLAND

British
Landing

LAKE
HURON

Sugar
Loaf
Woods   Rock

Fort

2 kilometres
1¼ miles

Wharves

MICHILIMACKINAC ISLAND
Fort Michilimackinac was captured on 17 July 1812

134

CHAPTER TEN

Michilimackinac, July 1812

L ate in 1811, the 49th Regiment was ordered to Montreal. Brock's dearest friends, and the 41st, were to be sent home to be brought to strength and equipped. In anticipation, many of the officers of the 49th were on their way home on leave, expecting to rejoin the regiment in England. Brock was disturbed, because this left him with some of the 10th Royal Veterans and a few Royal Artillerymen. Some Royal Newfoundland Regiment of Fencibles were on their way, and he also had his militia. On July 20 he wrote to Prevost that he was not very "sanguine" about the militia. He found a "general sentiment prevails that with the present force resistance is unavailing." In a later letter he wrote, "Most of the people have lost all confidence — I however speak loud and look big."

True, while volunteers were few, most men stayed on their farms and claimed to support their administrator/commander of forces. Of the Americans in the province, only a few chose to return to the United States. The mood remained resigned. The flank companies of the Norfolk Militia refused to go to Amherstburg when ordered to by their autocratic tinpot colonel, Thomas Talbot, the founder of his own settlement. One source suggests that the refusal had less to do with the cause and more with the high-handed rule of their dictatorial leader.

By February 1812, Governor Prevost wrote that the Prince Regent had approved Brock's transfer to join Wellington. Brock had to refuse what he had so longed to achieve. Was he confident enough to know that without him the province would be overrun? Was his true reason that he would soon see action without having to make the long journey home? To Prevost he replied, "The state of public affairs with the American government indicating a strong presumption of an approaching rupture between the two countries, I beg leave to be allowed to remain in my present command."

A letter soon arrived from Prevost's headquarters in Quebec City. The 41st Regiment, Lieutenant Colonel Henry Procter commanding, would leave for Upper Canada as soon as they could prepare. The 100th Foot would be moved from Halifax to Quebec and replaced in Halifax by the 104th. The latter had been raised in New Brunswick and put on the regular establishment in

1810. The 49th, to Brock's relief, would follow the 41st as boats and equipment became available.

Brock already had a plan, which he had sent to Prevost in December 1811. If, or more likely when, war was declared, they should seize strategically located Michilimackinac. (The name had been shortened to Mackinac Island by the Americans.) Brock knew of no better way to bring the Native nations of the north and west to Britain's side. They had been struggling to retain their tribal lands against the waves of frontiersmen flocking in since the revolution. They would welcome some indication of help from the British.

In February Brock faced his legislative assembly. The members refused to invoke *habeas corpus*. They passed a new militia act, but would allow it to apply only until the next session. He wanted civilians who were training some of the militia to take an oath of allegiance, to weed out disloyal Americans. That, too, was refused. Like most high-ranking commanders, Brock had little respect for democracy, even the limited form permitted the Canadians.

Without waiting for Prevost to veto his hope for Michilimackinac, Brock arranged for runners to take a "CONFIDENTIAL COMMUNICATION" to the person known among the tribes as "The Read Headed Man." He was the fur trader, a Scotsman from Dumfries, Robert Dickson. At the time Dickson was known to be somewhere near the Missouri River. He knew Michilimackinac well, for he had once operated a trading post there. When the island was handed over to the Americans in 1796, he opened a small trading post at the St. Peter (now Minnesota) River near Lake Traverse, a camping ground for bands of the Sioux nations. Dickson's wife, *To to win,* or Helen, was the daughter of a powerful chief of the Wahpeton branch of the Santie Soiux. She lived on Drummond Island with their four children. Drummond was close to St. Joseph's Island, where the British garrison was under the command of Captain Charles Roberts of the 10th Royal Veterans.

Brock's message to Dickson was dated February 27, 1812. As war seemed probable, he needed "to ascertain the degree of cooperation which he and his friends might be able to furnish in case of such an Emergency taking place." He asked Dickson to report:

- The number of your friends that might be depended upon.
- Their disposition toward us.
- Would they assemble and march under your orders.
- State the succours you require, and the most eligible mode, for their conveyance.
- Can equipment be procured in your Country.

- An immediate direct communication with you is very much wished for.
- Can you point out in what manner that object may be accomplished.
- Send without loss of time a few faithful and Confidential Agents — selected from your friends.
- Will you individually approach the Detroit frontier next spring. If so, state time and places where we may meet. Memo. avoid mentioning names in your communications.

When Dickson's reply reached Brock at Fort York on July 14, the United States had already declared war. Dickson, however, had understood exactly what Brock intended. He replied to the message on June 18, the very day the war officially began, news that reached Brock at York on June 25. Dickson had gathered together 250 to 300 "friends" and would lead them to Fort St. Joseph immediately. Assisting Dickson was John Astin, Jr., the storekeeper for the Indian Department at Fort St. Joseph. Between them they had gathered four hundred warriors by July 15 when Dickson arrived to join Captain Charles Roberts at St. Joseph's Island.

Roberts, too, was prepared. He had received a letter from Brock ordering him to take Michilimackinac as soon as he learned that war had been declared. Actually,

Brock had sent two other letters, the first asking him to forbear, the second telling him to use his own judgement. Brock had received another warning from Prevost to be cautious. A letter to Roberts from Prevost carried the same warning. Too late, this message reached Fort St. Joseph. Roberts knew the fort he commanded was even weaker than Michilimackinac. Should the Americans be reinforced, they could easily capture his post. He would leave only a caretaker garrison of six soldiers behind, taking every able-bodied man with him. He had no time to waste.

While Dickson had raised the Native warriors — Sioux, Ojibway, Ottawa, Menominee, and Winnibago — and about 180 Canadians, some of mixed blood, Roberts had recruited the local Nor'Westers and their schooner, *Caledonia*. The expedition set out on July 16 in canoes and aboard the *Caledonia* for Mackinac Island, a fifty-mile sail away.

Fort Michilimackinac was built of logs and protected by a lone 9-pounder gun. It stood on a limestone promontory above the harbour, at the southeastern corner of the island. Not far off was a higher hill with no defences. The garrison was of sixty-one United States regulars, commanded by Lieutenant Porter Hanks. They were unaware that their country was at war. Hearing of the large gathering at Fort St. Joseph, Hanks had sent a spy to investigate. This man was captured and taken aboard the *Caledonia*. Dickson and Roberts landed their forces on the northwest side of the island, out of sight of the fort, and released their prisoner. The time was three o'clock on the morning of July 17. The failed spy went among the inhabitants of the small village below the fort warning of the presence of the Native warriors, a sure way to spread terror. Meanwhile, some of Roberts's men hauled a 6-pounder gun to the top of the hill overlooking the fort.

At ten o'clock Roberts called on Hanks to surrender. Fearful that the Natives might attack in force, Hanks agreed. Next, Roberts's regulars and volunteers conducted a thorough search of the fort and outbuildings. These yielded stocks of flour, trade goods, wine and whiskey, arms, ammunition, furniture, bedding, and clothing, all removed and divided up among the soldiers, with Roberts entitled to the lion's share. The loot was valued at £10,000, which allowed a tidy sum for the participants.

Roberts granted the American regulars of the garrison the honours of war. They were allowed to leave for Detroit "on parole," which meant that they had pledged never to take up arms against Great Britain. Three of the prisoners were identified as deserters from the British army and detained to be dealt with later.

With the "bloodless capture" of Michilimackinac, the Provincial Marine, which Brock had done so much to create as a fighting navy, now had command of the lakes. At Kingston, a Scotsman and naval officer, Captain Hugh Earle, was the commodore on Lake Ontario. He had married Anne, a daughter of Molly Brant and Sir William Johnson.

At Kingston in Commodore Earle's fleet were:

- The *Royal George*, a corvette with twenty-two 24-pounder guns, the commodore's flagship, small but the only full-rigged ship on the lake at that time;
- The *Earl of Moira*, a brigantine, sixteen 24-pounder guns;
- The *Prince Regent*, a large armed schooner;
- The *Duke of Gloucester*, a large armed schooner;
- The *Simcoe*, a small armed schooner; and
- The *Seneca*, a small armed schooner.

Across Lake Ontario the Americans were hastily building a new naval base at Sackets Harbor, because the harbour at Oswego was shallow. The man in command before the end of the year would be Commodore Isaac Chauncey, experienced but cautious. Under construction was the brigantine *Oneida*, with sixteen 24-pounder guns, 243 tons, the flagship of the American fleet. A second ship on the stocks was the *Julia*, a large armed schooner with one 32-pounder gun and some swivels.

Also in the harbour were twelve small armed rowing schooners, top heavy with guns of varying calibres.

Within days of the declaration of war, eight small schooners set out to sail to Sackets Harbor from Ogdensburg, New York. They set out only to be spotted by Ensign Dunham Jones of the Grenville Militia from his home in Augusta Township. He gathered a party of enthusiastic volunteers, and armed with muskets and rifles they boarded some bateaux and chased the schooners. They isolated and captured two — the *Sophia* and the *Island Packet*. The other six succeeded in running down the river and back to Ogdensburg harbour. Jones and his volunteers towed the two captive ships to shore, removed their crews, and set fire to the schooners. This was a mindless gesture. Normal practice was to rename a captured vessel, hoist the flag, and incorporate it into one's own fleet. For the moment the six schooners remained under the protection of the guns of Fort Oswegatchie.

At Amherstburg the commodore was the Hon. Alexander Grant, eighty-five years old and ineffective. The acting commodore was Captain George B. Hall. The ships were the *Queen Charlotte*, a brigantine, and the *General Hunter*, a schooner.

The supply route up the St. Lawrence was precarious. The fleets of bateaux moved in convoys, with guards of regulars or local flank companies of the militia, to ensure that the Americans watching would not attack. One engaged in moving the convoys was James FitzGibbon, holding a temporary captaincy in the 49th until the company captain returned from his leave. According to FitzGibbon, the strings of bateaux hugged the shore. His account has been queried by those unfamiliar with the St. Lawrence River. The bateau channel was close to one shore for awhile, then moved to the other shore if that side was better. Furthermore, attacks from the many forested islands were a threat. They could conceal both smuggler and robber. At Ogdensburg, where the six small schooners were still sheltering, some of the garrison prepared to attack some passing bateaux. They met with such a hot reception that they soon abandoned the attempt and ran back into harbour.

On learning that the six small schooners were stranded at Ogdensburg, Commodore Hugh Earle sent the *Duke of Gloucester* and the *Earl of Moira* downriver to ensure that the schooners did not leave their harbour. Next, Commodore Chauncey sent a message to Sackets Harbor for the armed *Julia* to sail downstream and break the blockade. The three ships fought a battle above Ogdensburg. The *Julia* inflicted the most damage. When she had had enough she ran into the harbour with the other ships. The guns of Fort Oswegatchie discouraged the two ships of the Provincial Marine from continuing the fight. Afterwards the stranded ships awaited an

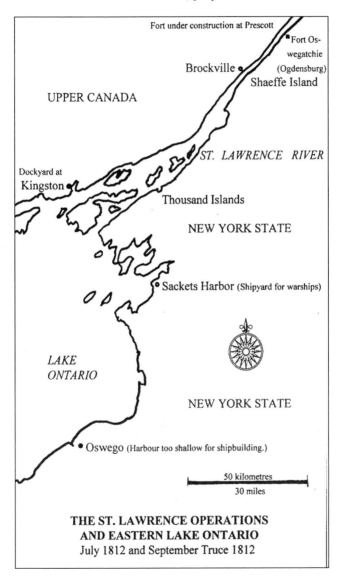

Fort under construction at Prescott

Fort Os-
wegatchie

Brockville

(Ogdensburg)

Shaeffe Island

UPPER CANADA

ST. LAWRENCE RIVER

Dockyard at
Kingston

Thousand Islands

NEW YORK STATE

Sackets Harbor (Shipyard for warships)

*LAKE
ONTARIO*

NEW YORK STATE

Oswego (Harbour too shallow for shipbuilding.)

50 kilometres

30 miles

**THE ST. LAWRENCE OPERATIONS
AND EASTERN LAKE ONTARIO**
July 1812 and September Truce 1812

opportunity to escape. This episode brought home to Brock the fragility of his main supply line.

Others escorting bateaux also had encounters with the enemy, some evaded, some not so fortunate. One American account recalls the capture of bateaux that had tied up for the night at Simmons Landing. The author must have meant Rockport, which at the time may have been called Simmons Landing. The family that had received the Loyalist land grant there was named Seaman — close enough.

About this time the British government had agreed to a conditional repeal of the Orders-in-Council that supposedly were the main cause of the United States' declaration of war. On June 23, 1812, the orders were officially repealed. However, as former president Jefferson was famous for saying, taking Canada would be "a mere matter of marching." Maritime rights were only the excuse; the real motive behind continuing the war was the elimination of all traces of the British presence from North America. First, they wanted Upper Canada, where they accused the British of aiding the Natives. Next they would target Lower Canada, and finally Nova Scotia to secure the naval base at Halifax.

Meanwhile, as the summer was passing, Brock was still at York. Long before the news of the fall of Michilimackinac reached him on July 29, his other preparations were well advanced. Some of the 49th had followed the 41st. With Lieutenant Colonel John Vincent, they had reached Kingston. Vincent had promised Brock that four companies would remain at Kingston, while the other six would be sent for service at York or on the Niagara frontier, the most vulnerable sector.

Owing to the dearth of officers of the 49th, Prevost was sending any who could be spared from their own regiments. Lieutenant Colonel Christopher Myers arrived, and Brock sent him to the Niagara frontier. Major General Roger Sheaffe, back from leave in England, would shortly depart for the upper country. As soon as he arrived Brock wanted him to take command at Fort George. He still had reservations about Sheaffe, but he had some strong qualities and he knew that area well. Brock's letters show a softening attitude towards Sheaffe.

The garrison at Amherstburg had a lucky break on July 2, when a longboat commanded by Lieutenant Frederic Rolette of the Provincial Marine captured the schooner *Cuyahoga* with American soldiers and baggage aboard. The captain, Luther Chapin, had not heard that war had been declared. Among the baggage, Rolette's crew found two trunks belonging to General William Hull, the governor of Michigan Territory and the commander of what the Americans called their army of the west. Inside one trunk were Hull's personal papers, letters to and from the Secretary of War

147

in Washington, and his own plans for invading Upper Canada. All this information was sent off by fast express to Brock at York.

Before the news from Michilimackinac reached him, Brock was almost resigned to having the Americans occupy Amherstburg and cut off Lake Erie. Now he learned that General Hull, whose base was at Detroit, had crossed the Detroit River and, on July 12, taken possession of Sandwich. There Hull issued a boastful proclamation that he had come with an army of friends, as a liberator:

> You will be emancipated from Tyranny and oppression and restored to the dignified station as freemen … If, contrary to the expectation of my country, you should take part in the approaching contest, you will be considered and treated as enemies, and the horrors and calamities of war will Stalk before you.

In fact, Hull had only four hundred United States regulars; the others were mostly Ohio volunteers, enthusiastic but untrained. Some fifty who were mounted were foraging through the countryside. Demanding people's food supplies was not the best way to win friends. On July 27, Lieutenant Colonel Thomas Bligh St. George, commandant at Fort Malden, wrote Brock, who was temporarily at Fort George, that his militiamen were drifting home. He had only 471 left at Amherstburg.

Brock had sent most of the 41st Regiment with Lieutenant Colonel Henry Procter to Amherstburg, where Fort Malden watched over the narrow Detroit River, which led into Lake Erie. Procter was to take over command from the elderly St. George. Brock's instructions were to prepare the best possible defence at both fort and town.

Informers were reporting to Brock on the conduct of Brigadier Hull and the United States Army at Sandwich, a village almost opposite fort and town at Detroit. After the news of Michilimackinac came word that Hull would soon have his regulars and militia in position to attack Amherstburg. Like many of the high-ranking American officers, Hull was getting on in years. The United States had declared war without thinking about the means. Officers who had served well during the American Revolution were still in command, and past their best. The country lacked a properly trained army.

On August 5, Brock prorogued the legislature. The assemblymen were droning on about a school bill instead of discussing war measures. However, the executive council agreed to impose martial law — military government — if necessary. Earlier, Brock had written Prevost that ordering martial law would turn the militia against him. Now that had changed. Because the victory at Michilimackinac had raised morale, Brock might get his way without making use of martial law. As matters turned out, Upper Canada was defended without imposing so draconian a measure.

Word came from the northwest of Indian tribes rising in support of the bloodless victory at Michilimackinac. The Iroquois nations were softening their stance and might be called upon to help, now that an American army was actually in the province. Leaders of the Iroquois would be John, a son of Joseph Brant, the legendary military leader of the American Revolutionary War days. Their most active leader was John Norton, a Scot, who claimed to have a Cherokee mother. He was employed by the Indian Department and had been adopted by the Mohawk people.

Brock resolved to set off himself for Amherstburg by way of Long Point on Lake Erie. At that rendezvous he expected to muster reinforcements. He wanted to be on the spot in person; he was uneasy that Procter might take too long over details and needed a good push.

Major Glegg was with him, and a new man, John Macdonell (of the Greenfield branch of the clan), who was born in Glengarry, Scotland, and raised in Glengarry County. Macdonell was a lawyer in York and a lieutenant colonel of militia. At twenty-six he was also acting attorney general of Upper Canada. Brock appointed him his

PADC — provincial aide-de-camp. With them went Brock's other PADC, Major James Givins, who had served in Upper Canada since the beginning of the American Revolution, and with the Indian Department since 1797.

Their journey began by ship to Fort George, followed by a ride over the portage road to Chippawa, where the armed schooner *Nancy* (possibly a renamed *Cuyahoga*) would carry them to Long Point. He brought some militia with him from York, and some well-worn red coats left over from refitting the 41st Regiment. He was taking many fewer men than had volunteered. Now that they had become enthusiastic, Brock made them responsible for safeguarding York during him absence.

Dedicated to the welfare of York was the new rector of St. James, the Reverend John Strachan. He had left Cornwall with his family in June, arriving much surprised to discover that war had been declared. He was puzzled that he had not seen enemy boats on the St. Lawrence (not even the *Julia*). The churchman was more than willing to bear arms himself in the defence of His Majesty's provinces.

CHAPTER ELEVEN

Brock and Tecumseh

Before setting out for Amherstburg, Brock had published his proclamation — big and loud — to counter Hull's:

> Every Canadian freeholder is by deliberate choice bound by the most solemn Oaths to defend the Monarchy as well as his own property: to shrink from that engagement is a Treason not to be forgiven; let no Man suppose that if in this unexpected struggle his Majesties Arms should be compelled to yield to an overwhelming force, that the settlers, the intrinsic value of its Commerce and the pretensions of its powerful rival to repossess the Canadas are pledges that no

peace will be established between the United States and Great Britain and Ireland, of which the restoration of these Provinces does not make the most prominent condition.

With the arrival of Lieutenant Colonel Procter and his detachment of the 41st, the garrison at Amherstburg now

Sergeant of the 41st Regiment on duty at Fort George. The coat is scarlet; the facings are the same, known as "red on red." Where the colours are both the same, the sergeant's sash has a white strip along the middle. Posing for tourists' photographs is part of the job.

consisted of about 30 officers and men of the Royal Artillery, their red coats faced blue; 250 of the 41st Foot, coats "red on red"; 50 Royal Newfoundland Fencibles, with the blue facings of a royal regiment; and 400 militia.

Fort George. Interior of a barracks room where enlisted men of the garrison lived.

In the town or the woods on both sides of the Detroit River were between four hundred and five hundred Native warriors, many naked but for breech-cloth and war paint. With the last were several chiefs, but the leader of their "confederacy" was the Shawnee Tecumseh. He had been leading his force in skirmishes across the river, and in attacks on wagon trains of supplies and militia, making for Detroit.

Tecumseh and his followers had become convinced that their best hope for driving back the waves of frontiersmen swarming into their hunting grounds was to join the British and Canadians. He made his decision following the Battle of Tippecanoe, about fifty miles west of Fort Wayne, on November 7, 1811. It was fought under the command of Tecumseh's younger brother, known as the Prophet. The nickname derived from a form of religion he preached. Since the Indian nations held their land in common, individuals did not have the right to sell off portions. Governor William Henry Harrison, of the Indiana Territory, claimed Tippecanoe as a victory for the white residents. In fact, it was indecisive. Harrison, as Tecumseh knew, wanted to see the territory become a state. For that he required a population of sixty thousand, Native nations excluded. He would keep the pressure on the tribes until he got what he wanted. Tecumseh had come to aid Lieutenant Colonel Procter by harrying General Hull's army.

Procter had sent Captain Peter Chambers with a party of the 41st to Moraviantown, a village of the Delaware nation, to rally the militia in that neighbourhood. Because they were behind Hull at Sandwich, they were in a position to prevent Hull from advancing up the Thames River. Hull was wondering what to do next. He wanted to hold both sides of the Detroit River to stop the traffic, but he was unsure how to achieve his objective. He knew that the Provincial Marine could bombard supply trains that had to pass along a road visible from the water.

The banks along both sides of the Detroit River were occupied by strip farms similar to those found in Lower Canada. They denoted the French-speaking farmers who had begun settling there in the 1740s and '50s. By the 1800s, some were fur traders living in Amherstburg. They were not interested in fostering British objectives, but they had no use for American frontiersmen, and those living in Canadian territory had no desire to be incorporated into the United States.

The first casualties for the Amherstburg garrison occurred in late July when a small party of Hull's army advanced and was halted by a bridge over the Rivière aux Canards. Standing on the bridge were two sentries, John Dean and James Hancock of the 41st Foot. The American Colonel Lewis Cass of the militia and James Miller of the regulars expected the sentries to take to their heels. That would have been the reaction of their own men, but not of Dean and Hancock. Both had been thoroughly drilled to stand their ground. Dean, arm broken by a musket ball, could still drive forward with his bayonet. Hancock, mortally wounded and bleeding profusely, fought on his knees until he collapsed.

The Americans then held the bridge, ready for Hull to begin moving his army forward. Hull refused to budge. He decided to wait for the arrival of heavy artillery, though he probably knew that few such guns were available except at Fort Detroit.

Hull and his army wanted to take Amherstburg because Fort Malden was the headquarters of the Indian Department. In command were Matthew Elliott, Thomas McKee, and the redoubtable Simon Girty (known to American frontiersmen as "the white savage"). All were stalwarts, related by blood or adoption to the tribes; all had been with the Indian Department since the revolution. The Americans wanted to close down the Indian Department, expecting they could neutralize the Native nations once they were cut off from British trade goods and presents.

Brock was determined not to lose Amherstburg for the same reason. By August 5, the day he left York, a supply train was making for Detroit. Scouting to protect it was a detachment of mounted American rangers. At dawn, they reached the Wyandot nation's village of

Maguaga. They found it deserted because Tecumseh and Matthew Elliott were planning an ambush. They struck quickly and faded back into fields of tall corn. Further on lay Brownstown, separated from Tecumseh and his followers by Brownsville Creek. Alexander, Matthew Elliott's son, was now at Tecumseh's side. The warriors struck again, scattering the Americans and raiding the supply train.

Best of all, with the baggage they found mail that revealed how demoralized Hull's men had become. A strong detachment of the 41st under Major Adam Muir, accompanied by civilian volunteers and militia, crossed the Detroit River to prevent the supply train from reaching Detroit. In a brush with the Americans, the 41st were badly mauled. Nearby, where Tecumseh was not in attendance, a young American was murdered to avenge the death of a chief. Among the volunteers was a fur trader, Thomas de Boucherville, who wrote how ashamed the white men were. Because the garrison at Amherstburg was weak, the British and the Canadians were unable to protest what they considered an atrocity. They could not afford to alienate their Native allies.

With Muir's small group of regulars near Maguaga was fifteen-year-old John Richardson, born at Amherstburg and a future poet and novelist. John's father, Robert, a Scotsman, was surgeon to the garrison. His mother was Madeleine Askin, of the fur trade family. Richardson had enlisted with the 41st as a gentleman volunteer. He had persuaded his stern father, a judge of the Western District as well as a surgeon, that the army needed him badly. His motive was to leave a school run by a sadistic master who made too free with the rod. Judge Richardson, on his part, was unsympathetic. He believed that plenty of thrashing was character-building.

Richardson was critical of the abilities of the regular troops against an enemy that took cover in the forest. "Here it was that we had first an opportunity of perceiving the extreme disadvantage of opposing regular troops to the enemy in the woods."

The regulars' packed lines and bright red coats did not work well in the gloom. They were no match for American riflemen, in grey woollen frocks, firing from behind trees. In the skirmish, Muir, wounded, had lost six killed and twenty-one wounded and taken two prisoners before he ordered a retreat to their boats.

General Hull was still at Sandwich. He had taken as his headquarters a brick house belonging to Lieutenant Colonel François Baby. Hull was still trying to decide what to do. British gunboats prevented him from sending his heavy guns by water. Then, on August 6, he learned that boats loaded with British troops (Procter and the 41st) had been observed following the Lake Erie shore, obviously heading for Amherstburg. More regulars, Canadian militia, and Native warriors would also be on their way. Hull felt he had no choice but to evacuate his entire force back across the Detroit River. By the morning of August 8, except for stragglers, the only Americans still on Canadian soil were those captured and held prisoner at Amherstburg.

By that day, Brock had reached Long Point with his men and supplies. He had brought as many regulars as he dared spare from the garrisons at Chippawa and Fort Erie. Most of his force had transferred to small boats for the rest of the journey to Amherstburg. All told he had in his party 50 regulars, 250 militia, and a 6-pounder gun they had taken aboard at Long Point. The crews decided to portage over the long spit rather than sail and row the long way around it. This was hard, time-consuming labour. While most of the boats were small, the flotilla was accompanied by the one-hundred-ton armed schooner *Nancy*. As with the others the men put their backs into dragging her across the sand. Further hampered by bad weather, the lead boats did not reach Amherstburg until just before midnight on August 13. Brock later praised the good spirits of all his reinforcements: "In no instance have I witnessed greater cheerfulness and constancy than were displayed by these Troops under the fatigue of a long journey in Boats and during extremely bad weather."

When the boat carrying Brock struck a rock, the crew tried to dislodge it with setting poles. Seeing them unable to push the boat free, the general jumped over the side and waded up to his waist. The others followed and lifted the boat away. After he climbed back up the side, Brock sent for the case holding his rum and handed every man a glass.

At Amherstburg, as they were climbing out of their boats, Matthew Elliott and Colonel Procter were waiting to greet Brock. From Bois Blanc Island, close to the shore, came the rattle of muskets.

"A *feu de joie* from our Native allies," Elliott explained.

Brock fixed a stern stare, drew himself up tall, and shouted, "We do not waste ammunition! Do pray, Elliott, fully explain my wishes and motives, and tell the Indians that I will speak to them to-morrow on this subject."

Late as the night was, Brock sat in Elliott's study with his aide, Major Glegg, reading dispatches and the material taken from Brownville. Elliott reappeared with a warrior who was, at five feet ten inches, tall for a Native. He was clad in fringed buckskin; three miniature silver gorgets hung from his nose. Around his neck, suspended on a cord or string of wampum, was a larger silver gorget stamped with the crown and initials of George III, signifying that he was an officer.

Many versions, old and more recent, recount the meeting of Brock and the Shawnee leader. Tecumseh supposedly cried, "This is a man!"

When Brock explained about the waste of ammunition, Tecumseh heartily agreed and said he would caution his followers.

From Brock's letters his nephew extracted:

> Among the Indians whom I found at Amherstburg, and who had arrived from distant parts of the country, there were some extraordinary characters. He who most attracted my attention was a Shawanee [sic] chief, Tecumseh, the brother of the prophet, who for the last two years has carried on, contrary to our remonstrances, an active war against the United States.[11] ...
>
> A more sagacious or a more gallant warrior does not, I believe, exist. He has the admiration of everyone who converses with him. From a life of dissipation he has not only become in every respect abstemious, but he has likewise

---

11. Brock was referring to the British policy of avoiding being dragged actively into the conflict between the Native nations and the Americans.

prevailed on all his nation, and many of
the other tribes, to follow his example.

Tecumseh had chosen to support the British after
due consideration of his options. If he expected his confederacy to be neutral, what would happen if the
nations that were traditional enemies of the Shawnee
nation chose to assist the Americans in the hope of
being permitted, as a reward, to keep their tribal lands.
Trusting the British more than the Americans, although
not by much, Tecumseh had brought his followers to
Amherstburg.

Allan W. Eckert, a sympathetic American biographer of Tecumseh, wrote of the Shawnee's first
encounter with Brock. Tecumseh expected to dislike
him, merely another "pompous governor-general" sent
by the British. Instead, Tecumseh saw a man after his
own heart. This man had the presence of a chief, a warrior, a leader in battle.

Eckert's description of Brock is not flattering. At
forty-three, Brock was a year younger than Tecumseh.
He was a physically huge man, six feet three inches tall,
with broad shoulders and hips, weighing nearly 250
pounds. His left eye was supposedly closed and he was
lame and walked with a cane, but his "afflictions"
seemed not to interfere with his "capabilities." (Eckert
did not give a source for this description.)

Pierre Berton, in *The Invasion of Canada* (1980), envisages him as "a remarkably handsome man with a fair complexion, a broad forehead, clear eyes of grey-blue (one with a slight cast) and sparkling white teeth." His word-portrait is based on Walter Nursey's *The Story of Isaac Brock* (1923).

Together, Tecumseh and Brock, two of a kind who favoured bold strokes over caution, began to plan their next move. With Hull now back in Detroit with his army, they looked in his direction. For the moment Amherstburg was secure. The best way to make sure it stayed secure was to remove the American army from Detroit. Nephew Ferdinand Brock Tupper recounted:

> Major General Brock enquired of Tecumseh what sort of a country he should have to pass through in the event of his proceeding further [towards Detroit]. Tecumseh, taking a roll of elm bark, and extending it on the ground, drew forth his scalping knife, and with the point presently edged upon the back a plan of the country, its hills, woods, rivers, morases and roads — a plan which, if not as neat, was fully as intelligible as if a surveyor had prepared it.

Brock was plotting, unable to sleep that night as his mind worked feverishly. Meanwhile, Sir George Prevost, now in Montreal, was doing his own plotting, seeking to prevent the Americans from invading by way of Lake Champlain. He would get in touch with Major General Henry Dearborn, whose headquarters were at Greenbush, New York, across the Hudson River from Albany, the state capital. Prevost would undermine enterprising officers like Brock to ensure that they did not endanger his carefully nurtured peace. Michilimackinac was a piece of luck, but such aggression must not be repeated. For now, though, Prevost was too late.

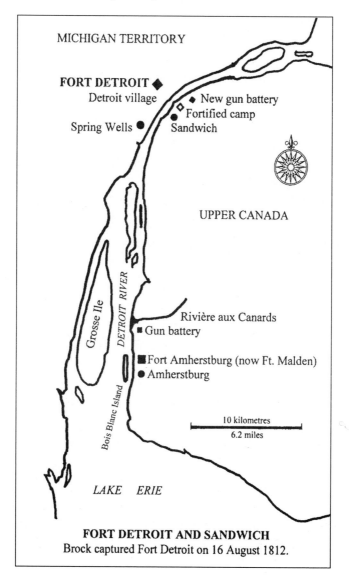

MICHIGAN TERRITORY

FORT DETROIT ◆
Detroit village

● New gun battery
◇ Fortified camp
Sandwich

Spring Wells ●

UPPER CANADA

Grosse Ile

DETROIT RIVER

Rivière aux Canards
■ Gun battery

■ Fort Amherstburg (now Ft. Malden)
● Amherstburg

Bois Blanc Island

10 kilometres
6.2 miles

LAKE   ERIE

FORT DETROIT AND SANDWICH
Brock captured Fort Detroit on 16 August 1812.

CHAPTER TWELVE

Detroit, August 16, 1812

Preparations for the drive on Detroit began in earnest on the morning of August 14, a Friday. With Brock on the scene, the morale of the Native allies soared. They complained that Procter had been too cautious, but he had reasons. He had no battle experience, and he feared losing any of the few regulars now at Amherstburg. Brock, with the joy of Michilimackinac to embolden him and taking full responsibility, was eager to plunge in.

Amherstburg, on the bank of the Detroit River, lay four miles upstream from Lake Erie. A battery now stood below the Rivière aux Canards, two miles north of the town and Fort Malden. The Detroit River was generally a mile wide, with some large islands — Grosse Ile (below tiny Bois Blanc), Turkey Islands, north of Rivière aux Canards, made good hiding places for both sides. Sandwich village was some twelve miles north of

Amherstburg, with a fortified camp built before Hull occupied the site.

In front of the Baby house, where Hull had stayed before withdrawing his troops, Brock's men were constructing a new battery. It was not detectable from the American side because it was screened by a grove of oak trees. When completed it would have three long guns — one 32-pounder and two 12-pounders. Some mortars, short, large bore cannons, could fire shells at high angles. From here, artillerymen could strike the village of Detroit, and after finding the right range, the fort.

The François Baby house (Sandwich, now downtown Windsor). The house was unfinished when General Hull occupied it in 1812.

G.R.D. Fryer

Plaque on the Baby house where Hull had his headquarters.

In the village were three hundred houses, mostly of wood. Many of the people were French-speaking. The site was enclosed on three sides by a fourteen-foot-high stockade, each side with a strong gate. There was no barrier along the water. On the high ground to the northeast was the fort — built originally by the French, rebuilt by the British, and now being repaired by the Americans. The fort was surrounded by a ditch, six feet deep and twelve feet wide, and two rows of pickets. These were pointed stakes, the blunt ends driven horizontally into the ground. Hull had plenty of guns, long 24-pounders placed to enfilade (sweep a long distance) along the road

169

and through the southern gate. Within the fort were more long guns, and mortars and howitzers, both short and firing at high angles. The fort, on high ground behind the village, was of stone, with a parapet eleven feet high and walls twelve feet thick. Hull had a formidable defensive site. Brock might be too optimistic. Yet here the Detroit River was less than a mile wide. The new battery above Sandwich was one thousand yards from the village and twelve hundred from the fort. Both were well within range of a 32-pounder.

Offshore, between Amherstburg and Sandwich, the river was controlled by the Provincial Marine. The schooner *General Hunter* and the brigantine *Queen Charlotte* were constantly patrolling.

On the morning of August 15 Brock addressed the allies — Tecumseh's Shawnees, the Delawares, Potawatomis, and now some Wyandots who had come across the river a few days before. About thirty Iroquois, no longer neutral, had also joined. Brock explained that he wanted the warriors to be at a safe distance but visible. If they kept circling in line past openings in the forest, the enemy would assume they were a much larger force.

Brock decided what troops he would take, and how they would be arranged. He would need 30 artillerymen, with three 6-pounder and three 3-pounder guns, the small ones for easy mobility; 250 of the 41st; 50 Royal

Newfoundland; 400 militia; and 600 of Tecumseh's followers. The total force would be 730 regulars and militia and 600 warriors — 1,330 altogether. Some of the captains would have local rank as majors for the duration of the operation against Detroit.

Brock organized his tiny army into three brigades. The first was fifty officers and men of the Royal Newfoundland Fencibles, and some men of the Oxford and Kent county militia regiments. The commander would be Lieutenant Colonel St. George. The second was fifty men of all ranks of the 41st and militia detachments from York, Lincoln, Oxford, and Norfolk, under Major Peter Chambers of the 41st. The third was the remaining two hundred of the 41st under their own Major Tallon.

To operate where needed were the thirty artillerymen and the guns. This meant three hundred regulars and four hundred militia in the brigades. Some three hundred of the militia would wear the worn red coats no longer needed by the 41st. This would account for American versions that claimed Brock had one thousand "crack regulars."

Lieutenant Colonel Procter would be in command of the entire force, "under the orders of the Major-General [Brock]." James Givins would be a provincial aide-de-camp, with the rank of major of militia, as a representative of the Indian Department.

Soldier-guide addresses "militia soldiers" in old coats of the 41st Regiment. School groups have the fun of wearing the type of coats used for some of Brock's militia in the attack on Detroit. With so many militiamen dressed in red, Brock fooled the Americans into believing he had "1,000 crack regulars" in his army.

Brock began marching his three brigades towards Sandwich. He ordered each brigade to keep a greater than usual distance apart to make his troops appear, from the other side of the river, more numerous than they actually were. Below the village boats and scows were being gathered for the crossing. Once the force was assembled at Sandwich, Brock gave his aides, John Glegg and John Macdonell, a special mission. They were to cross in a small boat, under a white flag of truce, with a letter from the Major General Brock to Brigadier General Hull:

Detroit, August 16, 1812

Head Quarters, Sandwich,
August 15, 1812

Sir, — The force at my disposal author-
izes me to require of you the immediate surrender of Fort Detroit. It is far
from my inclination to join in a war of
extermination, but you must be aware
that the body of Indians, who have
attached themselves to my troops, will
be beyond my control the moment the
contest commences. You will find me
disposed to enter into such conditions
as will satisfy the most scrupulous sense
of honor. Lieut. Colonel Macdonell
and Major Glegg are fully authorized
to conclude any arrangement that may
lead to prevent the unnecessary effu-
sion of blood.

I have the honor to be,
Sir, your most obdt. Servant,
[signed] ISAAC BROCK, Maj. Gen.

(to) His Excellency Brigadier Gen. Hull,
Commanding at Fort Detroit

Glegg and Macdonell were met by a party of soldiers who blindfolded them and escorted them to a house. There they sat, blindfolded, for three hours until Hull's reply was delivered to them. Back they were led to the boat and their escort. The blindfolds were removed by their own boatmen, who rowed them back to Sandwich. For all Brock had said about not using the Native warriors, he felt compelled to accept their help. They were his best hope for procuring a speedy surrender.

Brigadier General Hull's reply began:

> Head Quarters, Detroit,
> August 15, 1812
>
> Sir, — I have received your letter of this date. I have no other reply to make, than to inform you that I am prepared to meet any force which may be at your disposal, and any consequences, which may result from any exertion of it you may think proper to make.

John Richardson, volunteering with the 41st Regiment, wrote that the guns from the new battery began firing when Hull's letter reached Brock. In anticipation of a negative reply, soldiers began chopping down some of the oak trees that had prevented the enemy from seeing the threat. During the night of August 15–16, six hundred Natives crossed the Detroit River, led by Tecumseh, accompanied by Matthew Elliott in his role as a lieutenant colonel in the Indian Department. Little attention is given to horses in official accounts, but Tecumseh was said to be astride a white pony. They began circling the entire village and fort, passing gaps as many as six times. Many alarmed civilians with women and children had taken refuge inside the village, some in the fort, some inside root cellars.

Hull had sent a detachment of about four hundred men with Duncan McArthur, a general in the Ohio militia. They were to protect a supply train coming to Detroit by a trail, longer but safer than the road along the river that was visible to ships on Lake Erie. Now Hull sent a messenger to recall McArthur with all speed.

At dawn on Sunday, August 16, Brock and his little army boarded boats and began crossing to the area known as Spring Wells after the many local springs. Guns from the battery above Sandwich commenced firing. In his own memoir, John Richardson described the boats and scows and the canoes of Natives arriving after the first wave had gone the night before. The force marched along the shore towards the stockade around Detroit. Brock was in his scarlet "undress coat of a major general," splendid with gold thread epaulettes, gorget on his chest, and cocked hat. Was the hat old and shabby, or had he purchased one that only perched high on his broad head? He was portrayed as riding, which meant that Alfred, the horse given to him by General Sir James Craig, had crossed in one of the scows. Near him rode Lieutenant Colonel Robert Nichol, onetime storekeeper at Amherstburg, who was the quartermaster general of the militia.

"Pardon me, General, but I cannot forbear entreating you not to expose yourself thus. If we lose you we lose all; let me pray you allow the troops to pass on, led by their own officers."

"Master Nichol," Brock replied, "I duly appreciate the advice you give me, but I feel that in addition to their sense of loyalty and duty, many here follow me from a feeling of personal regard, and I will never ask them to go where I do not lead them."

When Brock was a mile away from the stockade, he called a halt so that the men could breakfast on rations they carried. While there, Brock learned that Captain Henry Brush, the man leading the supply train, had met up with General McArthur and his detachment. Now they were not far off. Brock had to make a quick change of plan. He had hoped to wait patiently for Hull to surrender. Now he had to strike before he could be menaced from behind.

Inside his fort, Hull dithered over what he should do. He thought mostly of the women and children who might be treated without mercy. The last straw was an 18-pounder cannon ball that bounced across the ground, through an opening, and into the officers' mess.

Present was Captain Porter Hanks, at Detroit for a court of enquiry into his loss of Michilimackinac. He died instantly when the ball struck him in the abdomen and cut him in half. Two others were badly wounded, while a second cannon ball killed two more soldiers. For the first time Hull learned that Brock was not about to cross the Detroit River; he was already outside Hull's southern gate. He decided not to order the men at the 24-pounder guns to fire. There was little point in giving the opposing troops further cause for revenge. He sent an officer, holding a white flag (really a tablecloth nailed to a pole), with a note for Brock.

The aides, Glegg and Macdonell, arrived for the second time under their white flag. Hull had asked for a three-day truce. Brock, the aides maintained, would allow him only three hours. Hull then wanted to protect Canadian deserters who had joined him. Macdonell angrily refused. What remained was signatures on the terms of surrender. Glegg and Macdonell signed for the British and Canadians. Colonel James Miller, a regular officer who commanded the 4th United States Infantry Regiment, and Elijah Brush, militia commander at Detroit (and uncle by marriage of John Richardson), signed for the United States. After some passing back and forth, the last two signatures, Brock's and Hull's, completed the business.

Brock, probably riding Alfred, led the way through the gate, the fifers and drummers piping and thumping out "The British Grenadiers." Some of the officers were members of the Upper Canadian elite — John Beverley Robinson, Samuel Peters Jarvis, Charles Askin, with his sister Madeleine's son John Richardson.

Despite Hull's fears, partly a tribute to Brock, Tecumseh and his braves marched quietly along with the cheering troops. Then suddenly everyone came to a halt and the British force was ordered to turn around and wait outside. Under the terms of the surrender, the American garrison and all the civilians were to quit the fort before the British and Canadian force could enter. When the fort had been vacated, Brock led his force in, regulars in the lead, red-coated militia next, followed by militia in green coats, then militia without uniforms. Tecumseh and the officers of the Indian Department marched last.

Hull surrendered his entire garrison, including Miller and McArthur and their four hundred men still escorting the supply train and Captain Henry Brush. Brock was still hard pressed to decide what to do with prisoners who outnumbered his own troops. Some sixteen hundred Ohio volunteers were sent home on parole, escorted far enough by regulars to be beyond attacks by the Native warriors. Hull and 583 regulars would be sent to Quebec City, the only place where so many could be accommodated. The Provincial Marine added the *Adams*, a sixteen-gun American brig, to the fleet and renamed it the *Detroit*. One man who had not left the fort with Hull was Private John Dean of the 41st, captured and wounded at the bridge over the Rivière aux Canards. He was waiting in the guard-room, where Brock sought him out. Both men took a moment to remember the slain Private James Hancock, the other regular who did not know how to run. Brock then secured the colours of the 4th United States Infantry Regiment. These he would send home as a trophy, perhaps for Winchester Cathedral, in honour of Guernsey.

Brock now issued a new proclamation to the people of Michigan Territory, who had lost their governor, William Hull. "Laws heretofor in existence shall continue in force until His Majesty's pleasure shall be known, or so long as the peace and security of the said territory will admit thereof."

Colonel Procter would govern Michigan as well as command at Amherstburg, as Fort Malden was a much stronger position than Detroit. Brock planned to hurry back to Niagara, taking with him most of the regulars. The next wise course would be to capture Fort Niagara, to prevent Americans from sending reinforcements to threaten the peninsula.

A first search through the fort turned up supplies that would be of great benefit to the defenders of Upper Canada. They were valued at $200,000, or £4,000. It was sufficient for every man to receive at least four pounds. Brock's share would be £214 to jingle in his often-empty pockets.

Brock had special words of praise for Tecumseh, whose leadership had been so effective in conducting the Natives according to the rules of war. The general took off his own wine-coloured silk sash and wrapped it around the Shawnee war chief's waist. In return, Tecumseh presented Brock with a woven sash of bright vegetable colours.

Brock's nephew Ferdinand Brock Tupper recorded:

> Tecumseh received the sash with evident gratification, but was seen the next day without the sash. The British general, fearing that something had displeased the Indian, sent his interpreter for an explanation. Tecumseh told him, that not wishing to wear such a mark of distinction when an older, and, as he said, an abler warior [sic] than himself was present, he had transferred the sash to the Wyandot chief, Roundhead.

Detroit, August 16, 1812

For Brock, the matter at Fort Niagara was now urgent. He would leave a few regulars at Fort Erie to support Amherstburg and guard the entrance to the Niagara River. While sailing along Lake Erie, Brock enjoyed discussing the coming campaign with several officers of the militia. One was Peter Robinson of the York Volunteers. According to Brock's nephew, Robinson recalled Brock saying: "If this war lasts, I am afraid I shall do some foolish thing, for I know myself, there is no want of courage in my nature — I hope I shall not get into a scrape."

CHAPTER THIRTEEN

Truce, August–September 1812

With the surrender of Detroit well in hand, Brock was in a frantic hurry to return to the Niagara frontier. With men he felt could be spared, he set off on the schooner *Chippawa,* now in the fleet based on Amherstburg, for Fort Erie. On the way, another new schooner, the *Lady Prevost,* fired a seventeen-gun salute in Brock's honour before sending him dispatches. For Brock the axe fell. He learned that Sir George Prevost had arranged a truce, an armistice, with General Henry Dearborn.

On August 1, a ship from Halifax reached Quebec with a letter from Augustus John Foster, the British minister in Washington, informing the governor that every effort was being made for a ceasefire. To placate the Americans, the hated Orders-in-Council had been revoked. Now there was nothing (except for American intentions to rid the continent of a British presence) to stand in the way of a peace settlement. The minister asked Prevost to lend a hand. Prevost sent his adjutant general, Colonel Edward Baynes, to Dearborn's headquarters at Greenbush, across the Hudson River from Albany. Dearborn, elderly and with little energy, happily signed. He was glad of any measure that would give more time for the Americans to reinforce their northern frontier.

Opposed to the truce was President James Madison. Orders-in-Council might be reissued at some later date, and the official cause of the war would return. Madison still wanted to pursue the ultimate purpose — to continue the war until the British were driven off the continent.

At Fort George, Roger Sheaffe had been in touch with the American commander at Lewiston, Major General of Militia Stephen Van Rensselaer, who wanted to ensure that the British officers would comply with the truce. Sheaffe, with Lieutenant Colonel Christopher Myers, commander of the garrison, and the Brigade Major Thomas Evans, agreed that no troops, supplies, weapons, or ammunition would be sent further inland than Fort Erie. Sheaffe saw this as a way of protecting Amherstburg and preventing the recapture of Detroit. He felt he had done well because he knew about Detroit, news that had not yet reached Van Rensselaer.

By the time Brock reached Fort George, on August 24, he was disheartened and furious. He had returned intending to sweep the Americans from their bases along the Niagara River, from Fort Niagara, past Lewiston, opposite Queenston, Black Rock, opposite Chippawa, and perhaps Buffalo as well. To his brothers, Brock wrote, "Should peace follow, the measure will be well; if hostilities recommence, nothing could be more unfortunate than this pause."

Meanwhile, word from the northwest was bad. Heartened by the success of Michilimackinac, some six hundred Potawatomi warriors attacked a column of fifty-four American regulars, twelve militia, nine women, and eighteen children. By order of William Hull, the group had evacuated Fort Dearborn, which guarded the village of Chicago, and were marching to Fort Wayne where they might be safer. In the massacre twenty-six regulars, two women, and twelve children were killed. Fort Wayne, on the Maumee River, was the only United States post left in the territories beyond Detroit.

To Lord Liverpool, the former secretary of state for war and the colonies, Brock wrote, with more discretion than to his brothers: "The Indians, who cannot enter into our views, will naturally feel disheartened and suspicious of our intentions. Should hostilities recommence I much fear the influence the British possess over them will be found diminished."

Liverpool had held the office until June. Appointed at that time was Lord Bathurst. Brock wrote to

Liverpool, who was more in touch with conditions than his successor.

During the truce, the armed schooner *Julia*, in Ogdensburg harbour, was free to sail to Sackets Harbor. The schooner had been stranded since the fight with the *Earl of Moira* and the *Duke of Gloucester* earlier that season. The six small schooners that *Julia* had come east to escort left at the same time, after having sheltered in Ogdensburg harbour since the war had been declared. American Commodore Isaac Chauncey ordered the schooners armed, each with a 32-pounder amidships and smaller guns along the sides. Whatever their names were before, they were now the *Pert, Growler, Conquest, Scourge, Hamilton,* and *Governor Thomkins.* Reports Commodore Earle sent reminded Brock again of the fragility of the St. Lawrence as his supply route.

After leaving orders for more work on defences and for more militia to be embodied and in readiness, Brock sailed for York. He left only hours later for a quick sail to Kingston. Prevost was angry that only four companies of the 49th had been left there with Lieutenant Colonel John Vincent. Brock wanted to see for himself whether the town was well protected. An easy route from New York State would be from Sackets Harbor to Kingston. An arms race to create bigger fleets for the control of the waters was on at the bottom of Lake Ontario. He still believed that the militia at Kingston and down the St. Lawrence was to be relied on. Thinking of his dear 49th, Brock felt his chest swell with pride. To his brother Savery, then in Portugal, he wrote: "Although the regiment has been ten years in this country, drinking rum without bounds, it is still respectable, and apparently ardent for the opportunity to acquire distinction."

With the truce, things might be going awry for Upper Canada, yet Brock was jubilant. He had been worrying about the dissent within his family on Guernsey. The members were estranged from one another, especially William and Irving, over the debts from the failure of the bank and business. Now he felt like shouting big and loud. He had the means to restore harmony among the folk who mattered most. When he had left Amherstburg his senior officers were still making inventories of the contents of the fort and village buildings of Detroit. Now he had the report, which showed that the loot amounted to between £30,000 and £40,000! On September 3, with time on his hands sailing to Kingston, he wrote the good news to his brothers. Part of his letter is already quoted. The rest introduced some new characters and mentioned many familiar ones. The letter also suggested that his attitude towards Roger Sheaffe had softened.

Brock to his brothers, Lake Ontario, September 3, 1812

You will have heard of the complete success which attended the efforts I directed against Detroit. I have received so many letters from people whose opinion I value, expressive of their admiration of the exploit, that I begin to attach to it more importance than I was at first inclined.

Should the affair be viewed in England in the light it is here, I cannot fail of meeting reward, and escaping the horror of being placed high on a shelf, never to be taken down.

Some say that nothing could be more desperate than the measure; but I answer, that the state of the province admitted nothing but desperate remedies. I got possession of the letters my antagonist [Hull] addressed to the secretary at war, and also of the sentiments which hundreds of his army uttered to their friends. Confidence in the general was gone, and evident despondency prevailed throughout.

I have succeeded beyond expectation. I crossed the river, contrary to the opinion of Colonel Procter, —&ct [by &ct, which means et cetera, he may have meant Prevost], it is therefore, no wonder that envy should attribute to good fortune what, in justice to my discernment, I must say, proceeded from a cool calculation on the *pours* and *contres*.

It is supposed that the value of the articles captured [at Detroit] will amount to 30 or 40,000 in that case my proportion will be something considerable. If it enables me to contribute to your comfort and happiness, I shall esteem it my highest reward.

When I returned Heaven thanks for my amazing success, I thought of you all; you appeared to me happy — your late sorrows forgotten; and I felt as if you acknowledged that the many benefits, which for a series of years I received from you, were not unworthily bestowed. Let me know, my dearest brothers, that you are all again united. The want of union was nearly losing this province without even a struggle, and be assured it operates in the same degree in regard to families.

A cessation of hostilities has taken place along this frontier. Should peace follow, the measure will be well; if hostilities recommence, nothing will be more unfortunate than this pause. I cannot give you freely an account of my situation — it is, however, of late much improved. The militia have been inspired by the recent success, with confidence — the disaffections are silenced. The 49th have come to my aid, besides other troops. I shall see [Lieutenant Colonel John] Vincent, I hope, this evening at Kingston.

He is appointed to the command of that post — a most important one. I have withdrawn [Major Charles] Plenderleath from Niagara to assist him. Plenderleath is sitting opposite to me, and desires to be remembered. James Brock [a cousin] is likewise at Kingston. I believe he considers it more his interest to remain with the 49th than to act as my private secretary: indeed, the salary is a mere pittance. Poor Leggatt is dead and has left his family in the most distressing situation. His wife died last year.

Major Smelt and Captain Brown have sent me your letters, for which I thank you.[12]

Let Richard Potenger [Isaac's sister Marie's son] be assured that his letter afforded me the highest gratification. I trust in Heaven that the whole of his thoughts will be directed to study and to qualify himself for the holy profession he has chosen. Ignorance is despised in most men, more particularly in the clergyman, educated at one of the universities, who must have neglected so many opportunities of acquiring knowledge.

I received the other day a long letter from Sir Thomas Saumarez, from Halifax. I regret the death of the two Harry Brocks.[13]

---

12. Major William Smelt, of the 103rd Foot, and Captain Brown were at Quebec, where the regiment was stationed.

13. One was Henry Frederick Brock, Esq., a jurat of the Royal Court of Guernsey. He may have been Isaac's elder brother, Frederic, who was born in 1768. The other was Lieutenant Henry Brock of the Royal Navy.

I have likewise been particularly unfortunate in the loss of two valuable military friends. I begin to be too old to form new friendships, and those of my youth are dropping off fast.

General Sheaffe has lately been sent to me. There never was an individual so miserably off for the necessary assistance. Sir George Prevost has kindly hearkened to my remonstrances, and in some measure supplied the deficiency. The 41st is an uncommonly fine regiment, but, with few exceptions, badly officered. [A dig at Procter?]

You mention John Tupper [a nephew, brother of Ferdinand] in a manner as to leave hope that he may still be living. God grant it! He is a great favourite of mine, and I should lament any disaster happening to him. Perhaps Glegg may be sent home by Sir George, and in that case I hope he will allow you to see the colours taken from the 4th U.S. regiment. The generality of the English will esteem them very little: nothing is prized that is not acquired with blood.

A postscript added on September 4 from Kingston read: "I this instant received your letters by Mr. Todd. So honest John Tupper is gone! I could not have loved a son of my own more ardently. Hostilities I this instant, understand are to be renewed in four days; and though landed only two hours, I must return immediately to Niagara, whence I shall write fully."

Anxious as he felt, he maintained a comforting glow. The prize money would help his family. Almost as important, he would now have the wealth to start thinking about a wife, not in this colony, but at the first opportunity to spend time at home. Like many officers before him, he would marry once he had the means to care for a family according to the standards in which he had been raised. For example, a former governor-in-chief of Canada, Guy Carleton — Lord Dorchester — did not accumulate enough wealth until he was in his fifties. His teenaged wife, Maria, bore him a large brood. Once the frontier of the Canadas was secure, Brock would think again of joining Wellington. With the fine impression he had now made, more rewards would come his way.

That was daydreaming. Back on earth he faced the prospect of outguessing the Americans on the far side of the Niagara River. How could he determine where the enemy might invade? He thought the best place was above the falls, where the land was lower, where they could easily set vast numbers of troops ashore. Chippawa, perhaps, or Fort Erie? Below the falls the walls of the gorge were steep, the current was much stronger, and the landing at Queenston was not spacious. Fort George would be the most difficult, even though the big guns were at Fort Niagara.

He had received more troops from Prevost, with the usual beseeching to avoid rashness, but still not enough. He knew that the men were spread too thin. He could not concentrate on any one place lest the enemy make a feint to draw his attention away from the real landing. Prevost had replied irritably to a demand Brock made in July. The 103rd Regiment had just arrived in Quebec, "about 750 very young Soldiers and Boys." Brock had no way of knowing so far that the enemy would help him at least as much as his own little army.

Major General Stephen Van Rensselaer commanded the militia. More militiamen were being recruited by Brigadier General William Wadsworth, of northern New York State. Of some six thousand troops gathering, nearly half were American regulars, commanded by the regular brigadier general, Alexander Smyth. Under American regulations, Van Rensselaer was superior to Smyth. The latter would have nothing to do with this arrangement, incidentally one impossible in the British army. A militia officer was always ranked below the regular officer on the spot. Smyth chose to keep most of his men at Buffalo. Like Brock he recognized that the best landing was above the falls. The mutual dislike would work to Brock's advantage.

When the news of Detroit reached London, Brock was granted his reward. The Prince Regent, acting on behalf of his severely ill father, King George III, proclaimed him a Knight of the Bath, Major General Sir Isaac Brock, K.B.

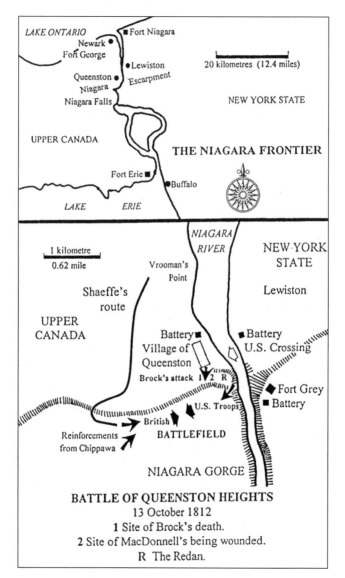

LAKE ONTARIO
■ Fort Niagara
Newark ●
Fort George
● Lewiston
Escarpment
Queenston ●
Niagara
Niagara Falls

20 kilometres (12.4 miles)

NEW YORK STATE

UPPER CANADA

THE NIAGARA FRONTIER

Fort Erie ■
● Buffalo

LAKE   ERIE

NIAGARA RIVER

NEW YORK STATE

1 kilometre
0.62 mile

Vrooman's Point

Shaeffe's route

UPPER CANADA

Lewiston

Battery ■
Village of Queenston

Battery ■
U.S. Crossing

Brock's attack 1 2 R

Fort Grey ◆
Battery ■

U.S. Troops

British

Reinforcements from Chippawa

BATTLEFIELD

NIAGARA GORGE

BATTLE OF QUEENSTON HEIGHTS
13 October 1812
1 Site of Brock's death.
2 Site of MacDonnell's being wounded.
R The Redan.

CHAPTER FOURTEEN

Queenston Heights,
October 13, 1812

Sir George Prevost was furious with Major General Sheaffe. In a letter dated August 20, 1812, he informed Brock that he was appalled at the arrangement Sheaffe had made with Major General Stephen Van Rensselaer. He had hoped the truce would make possible the strengthening of Amherstburg and Fort Malden. Prevost had not yet learned of the capture of Detroit. Nor did he know that the loot taken from the fort and village would greatly improve Amherstburg's stock of weapons and ammunition, provisions and furnishings, even medicines. The governor was especially angry that Sheaffe did not have his permission for his actions. Brock probably suspected that Prevost's real motive was to make certain that no one acted without his knowledge and consent. He also took credit for improvements, particularly the expansion of the Provincial Marine, that had been carried out on Brock's initiative. Prevost wrote to Lord Bathurst on August 17:

> The decided superiority I have obtained on the Lakes in consequence of the precautionary measures adopted during the last winter has permitted me to move without interruption, independently of the arrangement, both Troops and supplies of every description towards Amherstburg, while those of Genl. Hull having several hundred miles of wilderness to pass before they can reach Detroit, are exposed to be harassed and destroyed by the Indians.

After he returned from his mission to Dearborn's headquarters near Albany, Lieutenant Colonel Edward Baynes reported to Prevost that the Americans were poorly prepared. "His Majesty's subjects in both provinces are beginning to feel an increased confidence in the government protecting them." To the south, American militiamen were deserting in droves. Prevost continued, "I have thought it necessary to restrain Major-General Brock from adopting any measures he might judge fit for repelling the Invasion of the Upper Province & for compelling General Hull to retire from it."

Queenston Heights, October 13, 1812

The truce ended, as Brock had predicted to his brothers, on September 8. On September 14 he asked Sir George for more reinforcements. Prevost, who now knew about Detroit, declined. He suggested Brock might abandon Detroit and all of Michigan Territory. That way, he could withdraw troops from Amherstburg, rather than take any more regulars from Kingston. Lieutenant Colonel Vincent had sent twenty-five of the 10th Royal Veterans and the flank companies (light and grenadier) of the Royal Newfoundland Fencibles. The Veterans had proceeded to join the garrison at Michilimackinac, and the Newfoundlanders reinforced Colonel Procter at Amherstburg.

During this correspondence, Brock received reports on American strength along the Niagara frontier. General Alexander Smyth now had sixteen hundred regulars at Buffalo. Van Rensselaer had nine hundred regulars and twenty-six hundred militia at Lewiston, opposite the village of Queenston. On high ground at the south end of the village he had mounted two guns facing the landing at Queenston. Lewiston, Van Rensselaer decided, would be his jumping-off place. His regulars would gain a commanding position on the heights above Queenston — the famous Niagara escarpment, which at this point runs at right angles to the river.

In the village, Brock stationed Captain John Williams's light company and Captain James Dennis's grenadier company of the 49th Regiment. They were supported by two companies of the Lincoln militia, smart in the green coats of the citizen soldiers.

Most of Williams's company were on the heights; Dennis's grenadiers were close to the docks. Facing the river were two 3-pounder guns, nicknamed grasshoppers. Up the long northern slope was a small earthwork, a redan, where an 18-pounder had been mounted, far enough below the top of the escarpment to avoid being seen from the opposite side of the river. The gun was manned by eight artillerymen. North, about halfway to Fort George, at Vrooman's Point, a 24-pounder carronade had been mounted in a newly constructed battery.

The view downhill from Queenston Heights hardly matches descriptions written in 1812. The heights are the top of the escarpment, the unique feature of the Ontario landscape that attracts thousands of visitors each year. The top surface is of very hard limestone, or dolomite. The slope down is very steep. The land below is heavily wooded with large trees, a jumble of shrubs, and other thick undergrowth. To imagine a company of soldiers charging up that slope is difficult. There is a steep, winding path downhill to the edge of Queenston Village, with markers telling where certain events occurred, but they do not reflect the actual site.

One explanation for the difference is that Brock would have ordered a "field of fire." Enough undergrowth had been cleared to allow the crew of the 18-pounder a view. Some clearing would have made it possible, although not easy, for soldiers to claw their way towards the top. Today the land on top is a park with sweeping lawns and neat stands of trees. In 1812 the small ravines that descend to the north and east were choked with trees. A few small trails, known mainly to the Indians, wound their way to the top.

By October 9, Brock thought an attack was beginning. Lieutenant Jesse Elliott of the United States navy, leading some boats of American sailors and soldiers, boldly captured two vessels of the Provincial Marine almost under the guns of Fort Erie. They were the small *Caledonia*, the Nor'wester schooner from Michilimackinac, and the *Detroit*, the former American brig *Adams*. Elliot's men towed the *Caledonia* off to captivity. The *Detroit*, larger and unwieldy, ran aground and was set afire. The loss, especially of the *Detroit*, was the first threat to British control of Lake Erie, a serious matter.

By October, Brock was still waiting, staying at Fort George. He shared a small house with an old friend, Lieutenant Colonel John Murray, an inspector for the Office of the Military in Canada. During the day Brock discovered that some of his beloved 49th were causing trouble in Queenston. Wearied of doing duty in the little village, they were threatening to shoot their own officers. Brock sent his brigade major, Thomas Evans, to arrest the ringleaders, about half a dozen, and bring them to Fort George.

Evans was also to visit Van Rensselaer, under a flag of truce, to arrange to have the prisoners captured on the *Caledonia* and the *Detroit* exchanged for American prisoners being held at Fort George. On his return Evans reported that a crossing would be attempted probably within hours. He had released the rebellious men of the 49th, assuring them they would not be bored much longer.

Van Rensselaer intended to make his landing at Queenston, but he discovered that he had only thirteen boats — and no oars! He would wait until October 13, allowing time for oars to be found or made.

Brock was spending the evening writing orders for his senior officers, sending them to Queenston, Chippawa, and Fort Erie. Across from each post lay the American counterparts — Lewiston, Fort Schlosser, and Black Rock (north of Buffalo). Outside Fort George, he could hear the whoops of his Native allies at their campfires. Led by John Norton, John Brant, and Indian Department Major James Givins, members of the Iroquois nations from the Grand River had rallied to the cause.

Also present was a company of thirty black men, raised in St. Catharines by members of the Runchey family. All were eager volunteers, aware of the disaster American occupation would mean for them. They would be sold into slavery, from which many had escaped to sanctuary in Canada.

At about three o'clock on the morning of October 13, Brock was awakened by distant gunfire. Something had begun, possibly a feint at Queenston, eight kilometres to the south. He rose hurriedly, having slept, soldier-style, in his clothes. After giving Major General Sheaffe orders to marshal as large a force as the security of Fort George would permit, Brock mounted his horse, Alfred. He left with his two aides, Glegg and Macdonell, and a small party of reinforcements. Accompanying them were 160 Iroquois warriors. With the latter were John Norton, John Brant, and William Kerr, an Indian Department officer whose wife was Elizabeth, a daughter of Joseph Brant. From behind they could hear the guns of Fort George trading shots with those of Fort Niagara. The day was dawning grey and drizzling.

Brock galloped past Brown's Point, where some of his favourite militiamen, the York Volunteers, were marching for Queenston. This was the spot where he could have shouted the legendary words, "Press on brave York Volunteers!" John Beverley Robinson, then articling at John Macdonell's law firm at York, called out to Macdonell, who then left Brock's party to ride as the lieutenant colonel with the York men.

Soon, Robinson recorded, they passed some American prisoners being marched towards Fort George.

Around the landing was carnage. Some American regulars had crossed. Many militia had refused because they were not obliged to serve outside the United States. Among the prisoners were some from three boats that missed the landing and washed down the fast flowing Niagara River. When they had come ashore on the Canadian side they were promptly captured.

Brock, now splattered with mud, galloped into Queenston. He forced Alfred up the hill to the redan, where artillerymen were preparing to fire the 18-pounder. Above were Captain Williams and his light company. Brock ordered them down from the heights to join Captain Dennis's hard-pressed grenadiers, who were trying to drive back the landing Americans. From the redan Brock could see the battalions of the enemy. Now he knew that he was facing Van Rensselaer's main attacking force, no mere feint. He sent orders for troops from Chippawa and Fort Erie to join him.

Across the river, Stephen Van Rensselaer's kinsman Lieutenant Colonel Solomon Van Rensselaer was commanding the first assault troops of three hundred volunteers and three hundred regulars. Shot several times through his legs, he was now seriously disabled. His followers were soon halted by the fire from the light and grenadier companies of the 49th. During this American reverse, Captain of Regulars John E. Wool, of the 13th United States Infantry Regiment, had found a way to reach the heights. He led his own company, and some others, initially about fifty men, along a barely visible trail, slippery from the rain, but passable.

From the redan Brock heard the cheer rising from Wool's party, some three hundred feet above his head. Horrified that the enemy were actually coming down, he ordered the 18-pounder spiked and the artillerymen and redcoats to follow him as soon as possible.

As he ran down from the redan, leading Alfred by the reins, he shouted, "This is the first time I have ever seen the 49th turn their backs!"

Calling for men to rally round him, Brock waited until he had one hundred of the 49th and the same number of Lincoln militia. He had to recapture the redan before the enemy coming down from the heights could occupy it and unspike the 18-pounder. He gave the order to march: "Follow me, boys!"

He dismounted and tethered Alfred behind a stone wall.

"Take a breath, boys. You will need it in a few moments."

He had to act fast, and boldly. He knew he had scarcely enough men with him, but he had to try. Captain Dennis and his grenadiers, assisted by some of the light company, were attempting to cope with the steadily arriving Americans. He saw no sign of Captain Williams. Brock could not wait for any senior officer to lead the troops. And, after all, he would not expect his men to go where he did not lead them! The thought of Yankee woodsmen with their long, accurate rifles did not cross his mind. Like Montcalm at Quebec in 1759, Brock could not allow the enemy to consolidate on heights — nor in his own case let them control the redan.

A bullet from a rifle passed through his wrist, but he hardly noticed. A second bullet, from a sharpshooter skulking in bushes partway down from the heights, struck Brock almost straight into his heart.

Fifteen-year-old George Jarvis, a gentleman volunteer with the 49th, remembered the incident years later:

> Our gallant General fell on his left side, within a few feet of where I stood.
>
> Running up to him I enquired, "Are you much hurt, sir?"
>
> He placed his hand on his left breast and made no reply, and slowly sunk down.

According to legend, this was the place where Brock called out, "Press on brave York Volunteers!" Young Jarvis's memoir was correct. Of course, the York Volunteers were not far from Vrooman's Point in their march to embattled Queenston.

The attempt to charge the redan had failed. Brock was dead. His men continued their retreat, carrying their general's body. They sheltered from enemy fire behind the stone wall of the substantial house built at the north end of the village by the wealthy merchant the late Robert Hamilton. It was now occupied by his son, Alexander, militia captain, sheriff of Queenston, and member of the legislative council.

Lieutenant Colonel John Macdonell now arrived leading two flank companies of York militia. He attempted to retrieve the situation by rallying support. Still on the hill, concealed from enemy view, were Captain Williams and some of the light company of the 49th. With seventy-five volunteers, Macdonell reached Williams's position and the united force kept going. Ahead and above, Wool's men lay in wait.

"Revenge the General," came the cry for their much-respected onetime active lieutenant colonel of the 49th.

From his horse, Macdonell urged them on, until one bullet struck the animal, causing it to rear up. A second shot struck the rider in the back. Williams and Dennis, both seriously wounded, would survive. A dying Macdonell was carried north of Queenston to a house owned by people named Durham. He lay among the other wounded, British, Canadian, and American.

On the heights, Captain Wool was suffering from several wounds, the most uncomfortable being a musket ball through his buttocks. Taking command, the young Lieutenant Colonel Winfield Scott was ordering his troops to dig in and prepare to defend their position. Again the attempt to have a regular serve under a militia officer threatened to set back the defence. Winfield Scott, the regular, was outranked by Brigadier General William Wadsworth. He arrived on the heights, but unlike Stephen Van Rensselaer, Wadsworth allowed Scott to command rather than risk having him march off in high dudgeon.

All morning the gunners on both sides of the Niagara River had been trading shots. Around Lewiston, confusion still ruled, even though a large number of troops had managed to get on the heights. Americans now swarmed through Queenston. The situation was exactly the one Brock had feared, the one that had made him rush headlong at the steep slope. His action, intended to contain the few who had reached the redan, had failed. For men like Major John Glegg, Brock's aide, the worst had happened. The battle would be lost. Where was Sheaffe? What had happened to the reinforcements?

Major General Roger Sheaffe made his appearance at Vrooman's Point at noon. From Fort George he had brought three hundred officers and men of the 41st Foot, a "car brigade" of artillery drawn by borrowed farm horses, some Niagara Light Dragoons, Captain Robert Runchey's Company of Coloured Men, and more flank companies of the Lincoln and York militia. Sheaffe reconnoitred the land. No bold charge up the face of the

Niagara escarpment for him! In his book *British Generals in the War of 1812*, Wesley Turner personified Brock's leadership as "audacity" and Sheaffe's as "prudence."

On the advice of local warriors, Sheaffe examined the beginning of a long but not too narrow trail that wound the long way around to the heights, commencing behind Vrooman's Point. Sheaffe planned a lengthy flanking movement. During the morning the Americans on the heights had managed to bring up a 6-pounder gun and build some earthworks. Winfield Scott had sent men down to activate the 18-pounder in the redan. They could not dislodge the spike; in fact, a broken end of a ramrod had been well jammed in. Brock's artillerymen had done their work well.

Meanwhile, Sheaffe's regulars and militia continued their march around the scene of battle, approaching the gentler back slope of the escarpment. There they were joined by regulars from Chippawa. Out in front, the warriors led by John Norton acted as a screen and as skirmishers while Sheaffe formed his line of battle in a field belonging to a farmer, Elijah Phelps. Captain James Dennis had followed Sheaffe, wounds and all, with some of the 49th. The battle grew fiercer below the heights as two small guns placed beside the Hamilton house joined in the din.

The whoops of the Native allies were terrorizing even Scott's regulars. As Sheaffe's line marched into view, Scott looked about in despair for something white to wave. He attached a cravat — or maybe his shirt — to the tip of his sword, in surrender. Scott was quickly attacked by John Brant and one of his followers. He was rescued by John Beverley Robinson and Samuel Jarvis of the York Volunteers, who had joined Sheaffe's march after the disaster above Queenston.

Sheaffe and his senior officers had taken 925 prisoners, including Brigadier General William Wadsworth and 74 other officers. The Americans had suffered 250 casualties in dead and wounded. British and Canadian casualties were light: 14 killed, 77 wounded, and 21 missing. Most sadly regretted, most grievously mourned, was their courageous leader, Major General Sir Isaac Brock.

CHAPTER FIFTEEN

The Legend

The body of Major General Sir Isaac Brock was driven to Fort George, where the fallen hero would lie in state for three days. He was laid out, not in the coat he wore when he was killed, but in the older dress coat that he had worn as a senior lieutenant colonel and colonel and that had also served him while he was a brigadier general. The coat with the bullet hole would be cleaned up and returned to his family with his other personal effects. The epaulettes were dark, the buttons and gorget dulled. Tecumseh's sash would be sent home with the other articles. (The coat and sash are now in the Canadian War Museum, National Museums of Canada.)

Early on the morning of October 14, Lieutenant Colonel John Macdonell died of his wounds. By that time word of the passing of the much-respected and inspiring Brock was being carried by express up and down the roads

The coat Brock was wearing when the fatal bullet struck him. The bullet hole is visible almost in the centre. The coat in the portrait on the cover of this book seems to have been the dress uniform of a colonel. The coat shown here is the "undress" of a major-general, because the buttons from top to bottom are arranged in pairs.

and waters. A mood of despair and sorrow spread, while Major General Roger Sheaffe, who deserved some credit for winning the battle, was largely ignored.

Sheaffe, meanwhile, was mopping up. As had happened after the capture of Detroit, Sheaffe found himself with more prisoners than soldiers. Again, as after Detroit, he resolved to send only the regulars as prisoners to Quebec. The militia would be paroled to their homes. Thus the unwieldy number of prisoners was greatly reduced. Sheaffe had agreed with General Stephen Van Rensselaer to a three-day truce while everything was sorted out. He worked calmly and carefully, arranging burials and care of the wounded and planning new defences. Brigadier General Alexander Smyth was still at Buffalo with his regulars. He might already be planning a crossing. Sheaffe carried on, ignoring the widespread belief that only Brock was capable of saving Upper Canada.

The funeral was staged on October 16. Two coffins, Brock's and Macdonell's, passed between long lines of regulars and militia — muskets reversed — and Native warriors, five thousand all told. Minute guns boomed. From across the Niagara River, the guns of Fort Niagara joined those of Fort George, a tribute to a brave enemy. Another tribute was bestowed on the men of Brock's 49th. Americans who had faced them in the bloody battles through Queenston and the heights had begun calling them, after the facings on their coats, "the green Tigers"!

In all the reporting, no mention was made of Brock's horse, Alfred. If he had survived the battle, he would have been led before the coffin, Brock's boots set backwards in the stirrups. The bodies were interred in the York (also called the cavalier) bastion of Fort George until an appropriate monument could be erected. The bastion, newly completed, had been superintended by Brock himself.

Major John Glegg, the aide, wrote a lengthy description of the funeral to Brock's brother William. Glegg had arranged a simple ceremony, because he well knew his general's abhorrence of "ostentatious display."

When the news at last reached Governor Prevost, he was appalled, but, as usual, he reported briefly, ever mindful of presenting himself in a favourable light. Lord Bathurst, the secretary of state for war and the colonies, replied to Prevost: "His Royal Highness the Prince Regent is fully aware of the severe loss which His Majesty's service has experienced in the death of Major-General Sir Isaac Brock."

Word of Brock's knighthood finally reached Upper Canada not long after his death. Yet to be known was the Prince Regent's reward to Major General Sheaffe. In a few weeks' time, people would hear that he had been created a baronet, an honour higher than that bestowed on Brock. A knighthood died with its recipient, but a baronetcy was hereditary; it passed to an eldest son. If the Upper Canadians did not recognize Sheaffe's workman-like heroism, the home government did.

Many tributes to Brock continued in the days following the funeral. On October 24, the *Kingston Gazette* started the myth about certain last words:

> General Brock, watchful as he was brave, soon appeared in the midst of his faithful troops, ever obedient to his call, and whom [he] loved with the adoration of a father; but, alas! whilst collecting, arranging, forming, and cheering his brave followers, that great commander gloriously fell when preparing for victory — "*Push on brave York Volunteers,*" being near him, they were the last words of the dying Hero — Inhabitants of Upper Canada, in the day of battle *remember Brock.*

The *Quebec Gazette* for October 29 agreed that Brock had "given the impulse to his little army, which contributed to accomplish the victory when he was no more."

The Native nations held a general council of condolence at their Council House at Fort George. Present were Hurons, Potawatomis, and Chippawas, Deputy Superintendent General William Claus, Captain John

Norton, Captain J.B. Rosseaux, and others of the Indian Department. The chief speaker was Kasencayont Cayonga:

> Brothers — that the remains of our late beloved friend and commander, General Brock shall receive no injury, we cover it with this belt of wampum ... in conformity with the customs of our ancestors. For his successor, Sheaffe, five strings of wampum.
> — Sgd. W. Claus D.S.G.

Untitled and signed J.H.R. were the following lines:

> Low bending o'er the rugged bier
> The soldier drops the mournful tear
> For life departed, valour driven
> Fresh from the field of death to heaven
>
> But time shall fondly true the name
> Of Brock upon the scrolls of fame
> Upon the brow on one so brave
> Shall flourish vernal o'er his grave.

To one Private Flumerfilt, of the York Volunteers, was attributed "Come All You Bold Canadians" after the regiment returned to York. Set to a well-known tune of the day, the eight verses began:

> Come all you bold Canadians, I'll have
>   you lend an ear
> Concerning a fine ditty that would make
>   your courage cheer,
> Concerning an engagement that we had
>   at Sandwich town,
> The courage of those Yankee boys so
>   lately we pulled down.

The other seven verses and the melody can be found in Appendix B.

A song, author unknown, commemorated the battle at Queenston Heights. It was written no earlier than 1824 because it refers to the first Brock monument — "monumental rock." It begins:

> Upon the Heights of Queenston on a
>   dark October day,
> Invading foes were marshalled in battle's
>   dread array.
> Brave Brock looked up the rugged steep
>   and planned a bold attack;
> "No foreign flag shall float," cried he,
>   "above the Union Jack."

The other three verses can be found in Appendix B. Schoolboys at Chippawa used to sing it to the tune of "The British Grenadiers."

On the morning of November 10, 1812, the small schooner *Simcoe* approached Kingston. Led by Commodore Chauncey's flagship, the brig *Oneida*, the American fleet gave chase. The *Simcoe*'s captain ran her aground on a shoal between Amherst Island and the harbour, within range of the shore guns. The American ships paid off rather than risk being grounded themselves and pounded full of holes. Some shots hit the *Simcoe*, which sank while boats put out from Kingston to rescue her crew.

The *Simcoe*'s captain warned that the brig *Earl of Moira* was close behind him. In addition to American prisoners of war she carried, she was escorting a small schooner bearing the personal effects of General Brock, to be sent to his family in Guernsey. A fishing boat was sent to warn the *Moira* that Chauncey was lurking among the islands. Snow was swirling about. When it let up, the *Moira* found another brig rolling beside her. Its commanding officer demanded that she identify herself.

Recognizing that he was being hailed by Chauncey, the captain of the *Moira* begged the American commodore to spare Brock's possessions. To the chagrin of the prisoners, who were hoping to be rescued,

Chauncey allowed the *Moira* to go into Kingston harbour. Such was the regard for Brock that Chauncey was willing to await other opportunities to go after the *Earl of Moira*.

Fundraising and work on a monument to Brock began after the war. The monument was ready in 1824. The bodies of Major General Sir Isaac Brock and Lieutenant Colonel John Macdonell were removed from the York bastion at Fort George and reburied at the monument, with ceremony. In attendance were Lieutenant-Governor Sir Pergrine Maitland, KCB, members of the Macdonell family, and many colourfully dressed chiefs of the Iroquois nations from Grand River.

Meanwhile the myth grew, claiming that most of the credit for victories belonged to the militia. Sons of the United Empire Loyalists were righting the wrong done their fathers by the enemy. The role of the British regulars, who had in fact borne the brunt of the American attacks, was downplayed.

An enthusiastic proponent of the myth was the Archdeacon of St. James's Church in York, the Reverend John Strachan. The cleric became the driving force behind the establishment of the Loyal and Patriotic Society of Upper Canada for the benefit of the men who served in the militia but did not receive pensions. The society raised funds to assist disabled men and the families of those who did not return. Strachan visited many other towns and villages, opening branches to raise money to assist families in outlying areas.

Brock is remembered outside his province. In London, a tablet honouring him is in St. Paul's Cathedral, in the western ambulatory of the south trancept:

ERECTED AT THE PUBLIC EXPENSE
TO THE MEMORY OF
MAJOR GENERAL
SIR ISAAC BROCK
WHO GLORIOUSLY FELL
ON THE 13TH OF OCTOBER
MDCCC.XII
IN RESISTING AN ATTACK
ON
QUEENSTON
IN UPPER CANADA

No date for the erection is on the tablet, only the year 1812.

On Friday, July 13, 1969, an historical plaque commemorating Major General Sir Isaac Brock was unveiled at St. Peter Port Town Church. It was provided by the Ontario Department of Public Records and Archives, acting on the advice of the Archaeological and Historic Sites Board of Ontario.

The plaque to General Brock at the St. Peter Port Town Church. It was unveiled on June 13, 1969, on the advice of the Archaeological and Historic Sites Board of Ontario. From left to right are: W.H. Cranston, Chairman of the Historic Sites Board; Sir William Arnold, Bailiff of Guernsey; Mr. Allan Rowan-Legg, Agent General for Ontario; and the Hon. James A.C. Auld, Ontario's Minister of Tourism and Information

The plaque was dedicated by the Reverend D. Fenner-Smith, rector of the Castle and priest-in-charge of the Town Church, Guernsey.

Major-General Sir Isaac Brock, K.B.
1769–1812

One of Canada's outstanding military heroes, Isaac Brock was born on this island. He entered the British Army in 1785, became a lieutenant colonel of the 49th Regiment of Foot in 1787 and served in Europe 1799-1801. In 1811, just prior to the outbreak of war between Britain and the United States, Brock became President of the Executive Council and Administrator of Upper Canada (now Ontario) and rapidly organized the defence of the infant colony. His leadership culminated in the capture of Detroit and the defeat of the U.S. at Queenston Heights battle. He was mortally wounded during the latter engagement and is buried on the battlefield.

The 1960s were good years for Ontario history. People were awakening to the news that Ontario history is interesting and asking for plaques to persons of note in many communities.

The Brock family itself was interesting. Many other than Sir Isaac spent time in Ontario, including his brothers John, Ferdinand, and Savery and various cousins. Quebecers have those ten swashbuckling Le Moyne brothers. Ontarians have the Brocks.

CHAPTER SIXTEEN

Views New and Old

Some people, looking back at events that transpired nearly two hundred years ago, no longer see Brock as a hero. This is a pity. Canadians need their heroes — and need to know who they are. Now Sheaffe is receiving more credit as the winner of the Battle of Queenston Heights. But is Sheaffe a hero? The difference is charisma. Brock had it in abundance; Sheaffe did not.

One definition of a hero is a person who dies young and not in his or her own bed. This was Brock. Sheaffe died at age eighty-eight, in his bed in Edinburgh. He had two sons, both of whom predeceased him, so the baronetcy became extinct.

The temptation is to see Brock as foolhardy, that his dash up the slope towards the heights was not well thought out. Also, he was a large man, usually pictured in scarlet, bright gold epaulettes, flashing gorget and but-

tons, large cocked hat, and Tecumseh's sash. He was conspicuous and should have realized how conspicuous he
was. He probably did, but as he stated, he could not send
men where he feared to lead them. Think of the condition
he was in when he died; that made a difference.

After the mud-splattering ride on Alfred, Brock's
accoutrements were hardly shiny. He would not have
worn the sash he treasured when going into action.
Besides, the day was grey and hazy and rainy with no
sun to reflect off metal. Furthermore, a cocked hat
would make any officer a target; it would not automatically have identified Brock as the commander.

Riflemen, whether in the British or American or
other armies, were taught to aim for an officer's horse,
and then the officer, in that order. Pierre Berton saw
Brock as impetuous. Wesley Turner agreed that he was
bold when he served in Holland in 1799. At Queenston
Heights, Turner admitted, Brock had no one to dele-
gate to. Captains Dennis and Williams had their hands
full directing the grenadiers and the light company.

As stated in context, Brock's action in 1812 was
much the same as Montcalm's in 1759. In both cases
the enemy appeared to the rear. After weeks of pound-
ing the entrenched French along the Beauport shore,
the redcoats appeared on the Plains of Abraham. They
landed upstream at the place now known as Wolfe's
Cove and climbed up the very steep path from L'Anse

au Foulon. In the same way, Captain Wool and his infantrymen had found their path, and when Brock discovered them they were looking down and behind him. An unexpected surprise.

C.P. Stacey concluded in the *Dictionary of Canadian Biography* that without Brock's magnetism the province would have fallen to the United States. Certainly he was bold, but as Stacey wrote, "Boldness always succeeds when the enemy is ill prepared and irresolute." Conditions matched Brock's style.

The war dragged on until December 24, 1814, when it ended with the signing of the Treaty of Ghent. It has been dubbed the Treaty of the Status Quo. In his book *The War of 1812* Wesley Turner called it "the war both sides won." That is open to challenge. Canada was invaded; Canada, with the help of the British army, repelled four attacks, at least. Regardless of what the Americans say, they did not win! The treaty signed at Ghent changed nothing, except that Canada lost a tiny island at the foot of Lake Ontario. Carleton Island was claimed by the United States, but occupied in 1812 by two British soldiers and one woman. A few days after war was declared, a boatload of men rowed out from Clayton, New York, and removed the garrison. Carleton has remained a part of New York.

Sheaffe was Brock's successor as administrator and commander of forces in Upper Canada. Prevost removed him in June 1813 and replaced him with Major General Baron Francis de Rottenburg. Sir George informed Lord Bathurst that Sheaffe had "lost the confidence of the province by the measures he had pursued for its defence."

Rottenburg was an experienced soldier, but he was slow in supporting Procter when he needed reinforcements. During Rottenburg's time, the Americans attacked York, captured Fort George and Amherstburg, and defeated Procter at Moraviantown. In December 1813 Prevost recalled Rottenburg and appointed Major General Gordon Drummond, the commander who most closely resembled Brock. In *British Generals in the War of 1812,* Wesley Turner personified Drummond as "persistence."

Of the newer officers, two stand out by winning important battles in 1813. The first was Charles d'Irumberry de Salaberry, of a distinguished French-speaking family. He was also a professional officer who had served in the 60th Regiment and was a onetime aide to Rottenburg. When the Americans planned a two-pronged attack to capture Montreal, Salaberry was the lieutenant colonel of the Canadien Voltigeurs. He commanded both French- and English-speaking troops and Native warriors and won the Battle of Châteauguay. This was the only occasion where no British regulars, other than Salaberry, were present. As at Queenston Heights, the defenders drove off a badly led force, poorly organized, clothed, and provisioned, on October 26.

The other officer was Lieutenant Colonel Joseph Morrison, only thirty years old and in command of the newly arrived 89th Regiment. The lieutenant colonel had never been in a battle, and the rank and file were green recruits when they arrived at Kingston.

The other half of the two-pronged attack was to descend the St. Lawrence and join the troops marching along the Châteauguay valley towards Montreal. This second force, led by Major General James Wilkinson, was as badly led, provisioned, and clad as the one Salaberry subdued. Ordered to take part of his regiment, and two companies of Brock's beloved 49th, Morrison sailed in vessels of the Provincial Marine in pursuit of Wilkinson's much larger army.

The two armies clashed at Crysler's farm, on a piece of ground perfectly suited to the tactics of a British regular regiment — an open field enclosed by the St. Lawrence River, swamp, and woodland. There the disciplined regulars easily scattered a far greater number of Americans, who were not accustomed to fighting in the European style. Morrison and his 89th fought the following year at Lundy's Lane, where he was wounded.

By 1814 the American army was greatly improved. The old men of the Revolutionary War had been retired. Younger generals such as Winfield Scott knew the value of trained regular troops. William Henry Harrison, who succeeded William Hull in the northwest, was able to defeat Henry Procter at Moraviantown. Lost in that battle was Tecumseh, who died trying to turn back the enemy during Procter's slow, ponderous retreat up the Thames River. American soldiers were then able to put up a stiff fight.

William Hull faced a court martial when he was sent home from Quebec. Henry Dearborn, surely responsible for Hull's failure, presided. Hull was accused of cowardice and treason for handing over Detroit without attempting to defend it. The charge of treason was deleted, but he was found guilty of cowardice and sentenced to be shot. President Madison pardoned him because of his service during the revolution. Hull believed that in surrendering he had saved Detroit from horrific bloodshed and destruction of property. Had he been killed while resisting, he probably would have been hailed as a hero.

The loss of Tecumseh spelled the end of Native aspirations to prevent westward expansion of the United States frontiers. One televised version of the War of 1812 credited Tecumseh with the outcome of the struggles along the Upper Canadian border. Without Tecumseh and his followers, the United States might well have annexed Upper Canada.

During the attack on Toronto in April 1813, Major General Sheaffe left early, marching his regulars towards Kingston to save them to fight another day. Behind him, the surrender was left to the militia and the civilians. John Strachan, now the Reverend Doctor Strachan, took it upon himself to demand of the aged commander Henry Dearborn that the prisoners and wounded be cared for and the articles of capitulation be properly signed. He had the support of the York elite, many of them his former pupils in Cornwall. John Beverley Robinson, for instance, barely twenty-one, was the acting attorney general after the death of John Macdonell. Strachan was considered the most influential man in York and for some distance around.

James FitzGibbon, Brock's "favourite sergeant major," was promoted to lieutenant in 1809, and served as adjutant to the 49th Regiment. In August 1812, he escorted a brigade of boats from Montreal to Kingston, part of the way in full view of the American shore. In January 1813 he took forty-five sleighs from Kingston to Niagara. Whether he was at Queenston Heights is unknown. Records for September and October 1812 are not among the papers his granddaughter edited.

At the head of fifty men and aided by four hundred Native warriors under Captain William Kerr, FitzGibbon won the Battle of Beaver Dam in June 1813. FitzGibbon later confirmed that he had also received advance warning from Laura Secord. She reported overhearing American officers billeted in her home discussing the attack. After the war he was a career public servant, and in the 1820s

he became adjutant general of militia and served lieutenant-governors Maitland and Sir John Colborne in
many capacities. During the rebellion of 1837 he played
an active role in organizing the volunteers who turned
back Mackenzie's rebels on Yonge Street.

FitzGibbon had never fared well financially. In
1847 he left Canada for good. Lord Seaton (later given
a peerage Sir John Colborne) used his influence to have
FitzGibbon made a knight at Windsor Castle. He lived
comfortably and used his pension from the public service to pay his debts. While there, he had frequent letters
from members of the Brock family, and he visited St.
Peter Port at least once. He died at Windsor in 1863,
aged eighty-three, and was buried in the crypt of St.
George's Chapel.

As time passed, Sir George Prevost did not change.
He remained determinedly on the defensive. He missed
other opportunities when offensive action would have
made sense. While at Kingston in May 1813, Prevost
authorized an attack on the naval base at Sackets Harbor.
An expedition set out in three ships of the Provincial
Marine, but the breeze was light. Prevost decided to post-
pone the attack until the wind strengthened. Because of
the delay, the Americans had forewarning. The expedition
was able to set some warehouses afire and to recapture the
ship *Duke of Gloucester,* stolen from York the month
before. Without Prevost's interference, the attack would

have taken the enemy by surprise and destroyed the whole naval establishment.

By 1814 the war with Napoleon's France was drawing to a close. On April 11, Napoleon abdicated. For the first time, thousands of troops were available for service in the Canadas. Regiments of Wellington's veterans were sent directly from French ports to Quebec and inland.

From August 19 to 25, British forces attacked the east coast of the United States, captured Washington, and burned the public buildings. The badly scorched president's home required several coats of white paint to hide the damage, thus the name "The White House" was applied to the presidential mansion.

By September 1, Prevost felt strong enough to drive the Americans out of their bases on Lake Champlain, which would make Montreal less vulnerable. For the first time Prevost felt able to go on the offensive, reinforced by the regiments of seasoned veterans. He moved to attack Plattsburgh, New York, but even when he was so well supported he proved that, though he was good at conserving men and supplies, he was no field commander. He landed more than enough experienced veterans to overwhelm the defenders, but then he decided they should not strike until his fleet, sailing up the lake, could catch up.

He ordered the frustrated troops to withdraw, but the fleet never reached him. It was struck by the

American fleet and defeated. The outcome would have been a victory had Prevost allowed the veterans to take Plattsburgh and hold it. The situation called for a Brock, but the commander was the man Wesley Turner personified as "disappointment."

If Prevost had succeeded in capturing Plattsburgh, the peace treaty might have been more to Britain's advantage. Prevost's failure weakened the British bargaining position.

By the 1820s, steps were undertaken for a proper defence of Upper Canada. Construction began on the Rideau Canal and on Fort Henry at Kingston. Both are landmarks to be visited in summer. The Guard entertains at the fort. Boats of every size, from canoes to cruise ships, travel through the locks. Built to bypass the St. Lawrence, it is now operated as a national park.

Sir Isaac Brock's nephew, Ferdinand Brock Tupper, wrote two books, the second on Brock's life and correspondence. The first, *Tupper Family Records*, was published in 1835. After that date the author found the enormous collection of letters and reports he reproduced in his second book. In *Famly Records* Tupper quotes: "... the delightful village of Brockville, so called in honour of the late lamented Sir Isaac Brock. This enchanting spot united in its situation, every beauty of nature."

Further on he quotes from E.A. Talbot's *Five Years in Canada*:

Brockville was originally named Elizabeth Town in compliment to the general's mother, and the township or county, in which the village is situated is still called Elizabeth. [Elizabethtown was actually named for Princess Elizabeth, a daughter of King George III. It was one of several townships named in honour of the numerous children of the King and known as the Royal Townships.]

The hero's name is commemorated in Brockville, in the Township of Brock, and most recently, Brock University in St. Catharines, Ontario. Prominent in Brockville is a bronze bust on the green in Court House Square.

The most visible memorial is the Brock monument on Queenston Heights. The original, completed in 1824, stood 153 feet high. It had, for some Upper Canadians, become the symbol of the power of the Family Compact, or ruling oligarchy. During the post-rebellion era of 1839–40, border incursions disturbed the peace. Some were led by Canadian rebels in exile and others by mischief-bound Americans who called themselves patriots, or hunters. In 1840, in a violation of Canadian sovereignty, the top was blown off the Brock monument.

M.B. Fryer.

The second Brock Monument at Queenston Heights. The original, unveiled in 1824, was 153 feet high. It was damaged by a bomb in 1840 during border incursions that followed the Rebellions of 1837. The present monument, over 200 feet tall, was completed in 1853.

Plaque to Coloured Corps near the Brock Monument, Queenston Heights. This is one of many plaques a visitor can find. Others, for example, are dedicated to Major General Sir Roger Sheaffe and Laura Secord. A recent symbol honours Brock's horse, Alfred.

Suspected of the outrage was Benjamin Lett, a follower of William Lyon Mackenzie. Lett was born in Ireland and was an Orangeman. Very secretive and obscure, he was often suspected of wrongdoing, but nothing was ever proven.

The oligarchy immediately began fundraising to replace the symbol of their version of "peace, order and good government" versus unruly republicans. The second monument, much grander than the first, and nearly half again as high, was finished in 1853.

234

For generations since, the site of the battlefield and the monument has been a popular place for visitors of all ages. Families may stroll, picnic, and read some of the many plaques and markers around the site dedicated to Roger Sheaffe, Runchey's coloured soldiers, Laura Secord, John Richardson, and others, including Brock's horse, Alfred.

In June the park is crowded with schoolchildren arriving by the busload. The favourite place is the monument, where long lines of young people stand patient-

M.B. Fryer.

Brock Days in Brockville, October 2003. "General Brock" reads thanks for the warm reception from the steps of the drinking fountain/monument. Brock is played by Peter Mitchell, who is a re-enactor at Fort George. The coat is a compromise between undress and dress. The sash round his waist is multi-coloured to represent the gift of Tecumseh to Brock.

235

ly in the sunshine. They await their turn to climb up the stone steps of the long, circular staircase inside the stone wall, for the fine view over the countryside and the Niagara River.

With such a vivid landmark as the Queenston Heights battlefield park, dominated by the two-hundred-feet-high monument, Brock can never be ignored. In tribute to his companion in the grave, the late singer and composer Stan Rogers wrote "MacDonnell on the Heights." He lamented that not one person among ten thousand would know the provincial aide-de-camp's name!

APPENDIX A

Chronology

1769–1814

1769	October 6, birth of Isaac Brock
1785	March 2, Ensign, 8th Reg't
1790	Lieutenant, 8th Reg't (not on Army List)
1791	June 15, Captain, 49th Reg't. Barbados, Jamaica
1795	June 24, Major, 49th
1797	October 24, Lieut. Col., senior by end of year
1799	Campaign in Holland
1801	Campaign at Copenhagen
1802	First duty in the Canadas
1803	Mutiny and desertions
1804	Executions in 49th
1805	October 30, full colonel in army

1807	Local rank as brigadier general, later confirmed in army
1810	Commander of troops in Upper Canada
1811	Administrator and commander of troops in Upper Canada
	Financial disaster of Brock family
	June 4, Major General

1812

April 21	Conditional repeal of Orders-in-Council
June 18	United States declares war on Great Britain
June 23	British government repeals Orders-in-Council
June 24	Napoleon invades Russia
July 12	Brigadier Geneal William Hull invades Upper Canada
July 17	Captain Charles Roberts captures Michilimackinac
August 16	Brock and Tecumseh capture Detroit
September 16	Americans attack British convoy on the St. Lawrence R.
September 21	American raid against Gananoque
October 4	Unsuccessful British raid against Ogdensburg, N.Y.

October 13	Battle of Queenston Heights and Brock's death;
	Sheaffe succeeds Brock as commander and administrator
October 14	Death of Lt. Col. John Macdonell, PADC
October 16	Funerals of Brock and Macdonell
November 10	Isaac Chauncey gains control of Lake Ontario
November 20	Major General Henry Dearborn invades Lower Canada
Nov. 28–30	Brigadier General Alexander Smyth attempts to invade across the Niagara River
December 18	French army leaves Russian territory

1813

February 22	Lieut. Col. George Macdonell raids Ogdensburg
April 27	Dearborn's forces occupy York (Toronto)
May 1–9	General Henry Procter's unsuccessful siege of Fort Meigs
May 25–27	Dearborn captures Fort George; Brig. Gen. John Vincent retreats to Burlington Heights
May 29	British forces raid Sacklets Harbor

June 6	Battle of Stoney Creek
June 22	Laura Secord's walk to Beaver Dam
June 24	Battle of Beaver Dam, FitzGibbon
July 26–28	Procter's forces fail to capture Fort Meigs
August 8	During the night USS *Hamilton* and *Scourge* sink in Lake Ontario off Twelve Mile Creek. Two of the schooners rescued from Ogdensburg, Sept. 1812
September 10	Perry defeats Capt. Robert Barklay. Battle of L. Erie
September 27	Procter retreats from Fort Malden
October 5	Battle of the Thames (Moraviantown), death of Tecumseh
October 7	Wellington invades France from Spain
October 25	Battle of Châteauguay, Lt. Col. Chas. de Salaberry
November 11	Battle of Crysler's Farm. Lt. Col. Joseph Morrison
December 10	McClure's forces burn Newark, retreat to Ft. Niagara
December 19	British capture Ft. Niagara, burn Lewiston
December 29	British forces burn Black Rock and Buffalo

Appendix A: Chronology

1814

January	American delegates leave for Europe to begin peace talks
March 30	Maj. Gen. James Wilkinson defeated at LaColle, Que.
March 31	Allies capture Paris
April 11	Napoleon abdicates
May 6	British raid Oswego. Americans capture Prairie du Chien; British retake it, July 20
July 2–5	Gov. of Missouri Territory takes Prairia du Chien, builds fort
July 3	Brig. Gen. Jacob Brown invades Upper Canada, captures Fort Erie.
July 5	Battle of Chippawa. Winfield Scott
July 11	British invade Maine
July 19	Americans burn St. David's, Upper Canada British take back Prairie du Chien
July 25	Battle of Lundy's Lane
August 4–5	American attempt to take Michilimackinac fails
August 15	Lieut. Gen. Drummond's assault of Fort Erie fails
August 19–25	British forces strike U.S. coast, capture Washington, burn president's mansion

September 1	Prevost invades U.S., reaches Plattsburg on 6th
September 3–5	British capture USS *Tigress* and *Scorpion* on Lake Huron
September 11	Macdonough defeats Downie in Plattsburg Bay, Prevost retreats
Sept. 12–15	British attack Baltimore
September 17	American sortie from Fort Erie against Drummond
November 3	Americans blow up Fort Erie, retire to New York shore
December 10	British troops land near mouth of Mississippi
December 24	Treaty of Ghent signed, ends war

1815

| January 8 | Battle of New Orleans, British disaster, but war over |

APPENDIX B

Songs

Come All You Bold Canadians

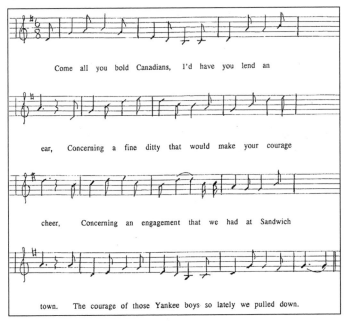

Come all you bold Canadians, I'd have you lend an

ear, Concerning a fine ditty that would make your courage

cheer, Concerning an engagement that we had at Sandwich

town. The courage of those Yankee boys so lately we pulled down.

2. There was a bold commander, brave General Brock
   by name,
   Took shipping at Niagara and down to York he
   came,
   He says, "My gallant heroes, if you'll come along
   with me,
   We'll fight those proud Yankees in the west of
   Canaday!"

3. T'was thus that we replied to him: "Along with you
   we'll go,
   Our knapsacks we will shoulder without any more
   ado.
   Our knapsacks we will shoulder and forward we will
   steer;
   We'll fight those proud Yankees without either
   dread or fear."

4. We travelled all that night and a part of the next day,
   With a determination to show them British play.
   We travelled all that night and a part of the next day,
   With grim determination to conquer or to die.

5. Our commander sent a flag to them and unto them
   did say:
   Deliver up your garrison or we'll fire on you this
   day!"

But they would not surrender, and chose to stand
their ground,
We opened up our great guns and gave them fire a
round.

6. Their commander sent a flag to us, for quarter he
did call.
"Oh, hold your guns, brave British boys, for fear
you slay us all.
Our town you have at your command, our garrison
likewise."
They brought their guns and grounded them right
before our eyes.

7. And now we are home again, each man is safe and
sound.
May the memory of this conquest all through the
Province sound.
Success unto our volunteers who did their rights
maintain,
And to our bold commander, brave General Brock
by name!

The Battle of Queenston Heights

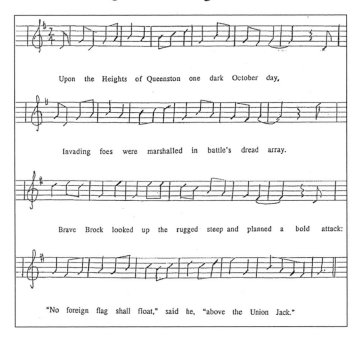

Upon the Heights of Queenston one dark October day,

Invading foes were marshalled in battle's dread array.

Brave Brock looked up the rugged steep and planned a bold attack:

"No foreign flag shall float," said he, "above the Union Jack."

2. His loyal-hearted soldiers were ready every one,
    Their foes were twice their numbers but duty would
        be done.
    They started up the fire-swept hill with loud
        resounding cheers,
    While Brock's brave voice rang out: "Push on, York
        Volunteers!"

3. But soon a fatal bullet pierced through his manly
    breast,
    And loving friends to help him around the hero
    pressed;
    "Push on," he said. "Do not mind me!" and ere
    the set of sun,
    Canadians held the rugged steep, the victory was
    won.

4. Each true Canadian soldier laments the death of
    Brock;
    His countrymen have honoured him in monumental
    rock;
    And if a foe should e'er invade our land in future
    years,
    His dying words will guide us still: "Push on, brave
    volunteers."

BIBLIOGRAPHY

The following list of sources shows that there is no shortage of material on this subject, either in primary or in secondary sources. There are even quite a few that are directed at younger readers. Why, then, another book on Brock? I felt that I could write a study on his life and times that would be a worthwhile contribution, something rather different. Of the many sources, details vary from book to book. I tried to take them all into consideration, in choosing the version I wanted to tell. One detail that may confuse is the location of the executions of 1804. Most accounts agree that the court martials were held in Quebec. That was true, but I conclude that the executions were carried out in Montreal. The main escort of the condemned men was the 41st Regiment, which was at that time stationed in Montreal. The commander of forces, General Peter Hunter, was too thrifty to move a whole regiment such a distance only to be witnesses to the killing of seven men.

Citing only primary sources is a favourite game. With Brock, this is difficult because there are hardly any primary sources that have not been worked over and over again. I thank the Priaulx Library of St. Peter Port, Guernsey, for genealogy of the Brock family. Some writers complained that Brock never revealed anything of himself. I think he did. From Ferdinand Brock Tupper's second book I included some of Sir Isaac's letters verbatim; let the reader decide.

Bibliography

Published Primary Sources:

Casselman, Alexander C. (ed.). *Richardson's War of 1812*. Toronto: Historical Publishing, 1902.

Cruikshank, E.A. (ed.). "Some Unpublished Letters of General Brock," *Ontario Historical Society Papers and Records*, vol. 13 (1915).

FitzGibbon, Mary Agnes. *A Veteran of 1812: The Life of James FitzGibbon*. Toronto: Wm. Briggs, 1894.

Tupper, Ferdinand Brock. *The Life and Correspondence of Major-General Sir Isaac Brock*. 2nd ed. rev. London: Simpkin, Marshall, 1847.

——, *Family Records*. Published by Stephen Barbet, New Street, 1835.

Secondary Sources:

Allen, Robert S. "The British Indian Department and the Frontier in North America, 1755–1830," *Canadian Historic Sites: Occasional Papers on Archaeology and History*, no. 14, 1975.

Begamudré, Ven. *Isaac Brock: Larger Than Life*. Montreal: XYZ, 2000.

Benn, Carl. *The Iroquois in the War of 1812*. Toronto: University of Toronto Press, 1998.

Berton, Pierre. *The Invasion of Canada 1812–1813*. Toronto: McClelland & Stewart, 1980.

Boorman, Sylvia. *John Toronto: A Biography of Bishop Strachan*. Toronto: Clarke, Irwin, 1969.

Carnochan, Janet. "Sir Isaac Brock," *Niagara Historical Society Publications,* no. 15 (1907).

Collins, Gilbert. *Guidebook to the Historic Sites of the War of 1812.* Toronto: Dundurn, 1998.

Cruikshank, E.A. *The Battle of Queenston Heights.* 3rd ed. rev. *Welland Tribune,* 1904.

Currie, J.G. "The Battle of Queenston Heights," *Niagara Historical Society Publications,* no. 4 (1898).

Dictionary of Canadian Biography. Toronto: University of Toronto Press

    vol. 5: Brock (C.P. Stacey)
    vol. 5: Craig, Sir James (Jean-Pierre Wallot)
    vol. 6: Dickson, Robert (R. Allen)
    vol. 9: FitzGibbon, James (Ruth McKenzie)
    vol. 5: Hunter, Peter (in collaboration)
    vol. 6: Norton, John (Carl Klinck)
    vol. 5; Prevost, (Peter Burroughs)
    vol. 6: Procter, Henry, (Hyatt)
    vol. 8: Sheaffe, Roger (Whitehead and Turner)

Dictionary of National Biography
    Isaac Brock; Daniel Brock

Eadie, Peter & Fionnuala McGreger. *Channel Islands,* Guide Blue, London: Black, 3rd ed. 1998, "Bailiwick of Guernsey," pp. 97-137.

Eckert, Allan M. *A Sorrow in Our Heart: The Life of Tecumseh.* New York, Toronto: Bantam, 1993.

Fryer, Mary Beacock, and Christopher Dracott. *John Graves Simcoe: 1752–1806: A Biography.* Toronto: Dundurn, 1998.

Bibliography

Fryer, Mary Beacock. *Our Young Soldier; Lieutenant Francis Simcoe.* Toronto: Dundurn, 1996.

Hitsman, J. Mackay. *The Incredible War of 1812.* Toronto: University of Toronto Press, 1965.

Kosche, Ludwig. "The Relics of Brock: An Investigation," *Archivaria*, no. 9, Winter 1979–1980.

Lamb, W. Kaye. *The Hero of Upper Canada.* Toronto: Rous and Mann, 1962.

Lossing, Benson J. *The Pictorial Field-book of the War of 1812.* New York: Harper Brothers, 1868.

Nursey, Walter R. *The Story of Sir Isaac Brock*, 4th ed. Toronto: McClelland & Stewart, 1923.

Read, David B. *Life and Times of Major-General Sir Isaac Brock.* Toronto: W. Briggs, 1894.

Robinson, G.W.S. *Guernsey.* Douglas David and Charles, Vancouver: 1977.

Turner, Wesley B. *The War of 1812: The War That Both Sides Won.* Toronto: Dundurn, 1990.

——. *British Generals in the War of 1812: High Command in the Canadas.* Montreal, Kingston: McGill-Queen's University Press, 1999.

INDEX

Index